COVERT CULTURE SOURCEBOOK 2.0

Also by Richard Kadrey

Metrophage

Covert Culture Sourcebook

Kamikaze L'Amour (forthcoming)

Signal: Communication Tools for the Information Age (co-editor)

About the author:

Richard Kadrey was born in Brooklyn in 1957, and now lives in San Francisco. He has no qualifications for anything he does.

COVERT CULTURE SOURCEBOOK 2.0

by Richard Kadrey

ST. MARTIN'S PRESS   NEW YORK

COVERT CULTURE SOURCEBOOK 2.0

Portions of this book have appeared previously in *Wired, Future Sex* and *Science Fiction Eye*.

Design by David Barker.

Library of Congress Cataloging-in-Publication Data

Kadrey, Richard.
    Covert culture sourcebook 2.0 / Richard Kadrey.
          p.   cm.
    ISBN 0-312-11255-6 (pbk.)
    1. Social history—1970- 2. Civilization, Modern—1950-
3. Subculture.   I. Title.
HN17.5.K332   1994
    306 1—dc20
                                  94-19686
                                  CIP

First Edition: November 1994

10 9 8 7 6 5 4 3 2 1

Acknowledgements

You'd think experience would make a book like this easier to do the second time around, but it doesn't always work that way. **CCS 2.0** wasn't harder than the first one, but it was *weirder*. That's the problem with ambition: you want to make the new book better, so you toss up more obstacles for everyone involved. Don't weep too much for us, though. Writing is better than real work, and I did most of my part in my underwear, which is pretty much my description of a dream job.

Once again, I'd like to thank David Barker for design above and beyond the call, and Ellen Klages for keeping my rogue commas and gift for amusing spellings under control. I'd also like to thank my editor, Gordon Van Gelder, for his godlike patience, and my agent, Merrilee Heifetz, for saving me from a life of crime.

I'm pathetically grateful to the many contributors who wrote some terrific reviews, came up with information when I needed it and basically kept me from climbing on the roof with a high-powered rifle and re-enacting my favorite scenes from *Targets*: Tod Booth, who was screwed out of recognition for writing the "Kung Fu and Beyond" section of the first **CCS**, Tiffany Lee Brown, Daphne Gottlieb, Daryl-Lynn Johnson, Paul Kimball, Steve Lombardi, David Memmott, Pat Murphy, Phil Rzewski, Miryam Sas, Lewis Shiner and Bruce Sterling.

This book is dedicated to my mother, Jimi Kadrey, who let me read pretty much anything I wanted as a kid (and let me get away with the kind of crap that no one but a nerdy only child would pull), and to Pat, who puts up with similar nonsense today.

Contents

An Introduction (with a Side of Clarification)

What you're holding in your hands is the **Covert Culture Sourcebook 2.0**, a brand new book, not an update, tarting up, or expansion of the first **CCS**, but a brand new work. What's the difference between **CCS 1** and **2**? Why should you buy both and make me rich (or at least able to afford a ring job for the Toyota)? To answer that, I have to admit a couple of things up front. The first **CCS** was written expressly for me, the me I was when I was 16, living in Houston, Texas, in the mid-'70s and going slowly batshit. I hated the music my friends listened to. I hated the books and zines they read. I hated the movies they liked. I hated their clothes and their dreams and their heroes. In short, I was a gnarled little mutant exiled in a humid cattle town and thoroughly convinced that I was the only idiot like me in the world. Eventually, punk music pierced the cultural haze that walled in Houston in those days. I saw Iggy Pop and the Dead Boys, found some punk zines from England and New York, and for the first time in my liquored-up-fuck-me?-hey-fuck-you adolescence, realized that not only were there lots of other freaks out there, but that they were just as gnarled and restless as I was. That's who the first **CCS** was for: that amphetamined teeny-bopper who was stuck somewhere he didn't want to be and needed to know he wasn't alone in his cranky obsessions.

Fastforward 20 years. Even punks grow up. Sort of. Some of us have managed to eat while avoiding real jobs for a few years, and become obsessed with new things. The first **CCS** concentrated on traditional media that anyone, anywhere could deal with: printed zines and books, cassettes, CDs, videos, etc. **CCS 2.0** moves further into some of the newer, more abstract electronic media: cyberspace, the World Wide Web, disk-based books. The zines section of the first book becomes a section on electronic zines (ezines) in this one. None of these choices are improvements or the Daring New Edge of Culture, they're simply more choices, more places you can go if you're not satisfied with where you are or what you're asked to consume by conventional media.

A Clarification: What This Book Is Not

I don't generally write letters to editors or answer critics, but I'm going to take a moment here to clarify some things that seemed to puzzle a few people about the first **CCS**.

This is not a rah-rah-underground-culture-rules book. It's an information guide, a big damned list (with addresses and phone numbers) of items that my contributors and I think you might find interesting. That's all it is. I have no intention of putting things into perspective for you. I have no interest in telling you what to think. This book isn't about that. It's not a how-to or why-you-should or a history of the underground. I'm not trying to show the relationship between the sparkling and brilliant baubles of the fringe and the waxy dreariness of the mainstream. This is a book about information, options and useful stuff that you can get your hands, asses or eyeballs on. Period. If you're looking for those other books, or think I'm a schmuck for writing this one the way I did, I have one thing to say: write your own damned book.

It's not that hard, really. In my heart of hearts, I believe that any reasonably intelligent adult, with a little help, can do what I did—and maybe do it better. Desktop publishing is not that hard to learn. And there's a big used computer market out there. Remember: there is no such thing as obsolete technology anymore. There's just technology that's considered uncool. One of the best books I found while putting together **CCS 2.0** is the **Offbeat Video Source Guide**, a guide to virtually every video distributor in the known universe. It's a book with a plain yellow cover, spiral bound, photocopied on white paper. It's not a pretty book by anyone's standards, but it sings beautifully, and it's one of the most useful video reference works I've seen. And author Dennis Murry did the whole thing on an old Apple IIe, (which is sort of like recording the new Madonna album with a straight pin and a wax cylinder), but he did it. Neither of us are geniuses or rich. If we did it, you can too.

One last item: in order to make both volumes of **CCS** useful for the long haul, I'm going to send free quarterly updates via email to anyone who wants them. All you have to do is send a message to the Internet address below, and you're on the list. Also, I'll be including some new reviews along with the updates, just to keep you amused. If you don't have email access, you can always send a SASE to the postal address and receive the same information. One envelope per update. Of course, if you have any praise, money, abuse or potential review items you'd like to pass along, you can use the same address.

Richard Kadrey
Gomi Boy Industries
2440 16th St., #229
San Francisco, CA 94103
email: kadrey@well.com

BOOKS

Nerf optique
Nerf moteur de l'œil
Nerf facial
Nerf de la langue
Nerf auditif

Introduction—Books

With the big publishing houses getting more conservative in the books they're willing to publish and with (relatively) cheap computers and pirateable desktop publishing software, small presses have become the kudzu of the literary world. Little regional presses are popping up all over the country. Small groups of like-minded punks, lesbians, libertarians, bird watchers, and tapdancing Buddhist anarchists are banding together, putting words down on paper and between two covers. Small press fiction, in particular, has always been daring, but recently its quality has been able to match its ambition. And we're not talking about vanity press stuff here, or some arch little poetry zine with a circulation the size of a high school swim meet. Many successful small press titles sell thousands of copies. Why? Because the micro-publishers only bring out books they believe in, and unlike the big boys, they keep the books in print. The wham-bam-thank-you-ma'am principle at work at the big houses often dooms certain books even before they're printed (a hint: anytime you see a major publisher print a hardcover short story collection by a writer who is not Stephen King, you can bet that the book is probably a pity fuck or the result of blackmail by the writer's agent).

CCS 2.0 takes a look at a nice cross-section of savory small press fiction. Since style and subject matter are wide open here, you can find something for virtually any taste, from the opium-languid prose poetry of Danielle Willis' **Dogs in Lingerie** to the Borges-in-a-cowboy-hat mini-fictions of Don Webb's **Uncle Ovid's Exercise Book**, to the surrealist science fiction in Neal Barrett Jr.'s **The Hereafter Gang**. Of course, a few exceptional titles from the big presses made it into the fiction section, too, but since this is my book, I figure I get to break the rules once in a while.

We also have reviews of some computer disk-based titles. These are a fairly recent idea. Most use a text-linking system called Hypertext. Instead of just taking a book and dumping it onto a disk (which is a pretty boring idea), Hypertext books allow you to click on key words in the narrative and get more information, or move to a different part of the story. It's a new way of reading and writing, an artform that's still under construction.

Like the first **CCS**, we also have a sampling of non-fiction books to feed your information and obsession Jones. Unusual biographies and conspiracy theories. Books on death, the body, the mind, religion and a section on *The Other*: our secret selves, freaks, misfits and strangers.

Remember boys and girls, if consciousness is the only thing that separates us from the animals, books are the thing that separates us from animals and Hollywood producers.

The Lizard Club

by Steve Abbott
$7; Autonomedia
1993; 159 pp.

A weird parfait of sex, autobiography, tall tales, cosmic theories, and lizards, with just a little bit of Abbott's poet-persona showing off its prose-slinging muscles.

The Lizard Club alternates between descriptions of contemporary San Francisco boho lifestyles—club scenes, art references and sexual fantasies whizzing by like bullets off Superman's chest—childhood reveries, newspaper excerpts, diagrams, interviews and lectures about the place of lizards in the history of the world. Not surprisingly, lizards are the dominant species in the book. We don't realize this, however, until the end of the first chapter when, after a morning of drinking coffee and reading *The Far Side* in the local paper, our hero chows down on his boss, Komodo dragon-style. The lizard metaphor/reality is in full swing from there, complete with lizard queer bars (where the go-go boys don't dance on stage, but in a green-lit pit) to lizard twelve-step programs (with uplifting saurian slogans such as "Just Don't Take The First Bite" and "It's Nuts To Eat People").

Lies, truths, pseudo-scientific theories and Burroughsian "routines" make this truly postmodern life story more entertaining than the straight truth or a fully fictionalized account could ever be (and probably gets a lot closer to the truth of the author's experience).

The Kafka Chronicles

by Mark Amerika
$7.00; Black Ice Books
1993; 189 pp.

William Burroughs grew up and started writing in an era of covert sex, jazz, drugs, rising U.S. influence in the world, and a social era that was the mythical height of the American nuclear family, while a growing artist underground was pointing out the emptiness of that family's existence. Mark Amerika grew up in an era of open, dangerous sex, rock & roll, drugs, and the crumbling of the twin pillars of American pre-eminence and the *still*-mythical nuclear family.

Perhaps the biggest dividing line between Amerika and Burroughs (they are working in similar areas of language, sexuality, and political outrage) is jazz and rock & roll. The opening of **The Kafka Chronicles** reads like a mixture of Burroughs and Céline backed alternately by the Ramones and Glen Branca. But don't let the comparisons to earlier writers put you off—this is no mere cover version of earlier hits. In **The Kafka Chronicles,** you can find a bridge between earlier text transgressors and their step-children who grew up in the gray streets they predicted and sometimes parodied, where sex and politics are linked by a bleeding umbilical and there's music in every room.

Griffin & Sabine

An Extraordinary Correspondence
by Nick Bantock
$17.95; Chronicle Books
1991; 40 pp.

The ultimate epistolary novel, **Griffin and Sabine** offers the voyeuristic pleasure of reading someone else's mail. Griffin Moss, an artist living in London, receives a postcard from Sabine Strohem, an artist who lives in the Sicmon Islands, islands so small "they're no more than specks of dust in standard atlases." Sabine claims that she shares Griffin's sight: when he draws or paints, she sees what he is doing. The "extraordinary correspondence" between these two artists unfolds in words and pictures, with each page of the lavishly illustrated book providing another postcard, another letter to open and read (literally: a letter with envelope and carefully folded missive).

In recent years, there has been much talk of *virtual reality,* created environments that people can experience and explore without really being there. The usual presentation of virtual reality involves computers and a great deal of sophisticated technology. **Griffin and Sabine** is a low-tech version of virtual reality. Reading the love letters between the artists, I had an oddly persistent sensation that I was reading over the shoulder of Griffin—or was it Sabine?—Pat Murphy

The Hereafter Gang

by Neal Barrett, Jr.

1991; 348 pp.
information from: Mark V. Ziesing, P.O. Box 76, Shingletown, CA 96088; 916-474-1580

Don't get the idea that I'm opposed to fine writing. *Au contraire*. I don't mind somebody being able to conjure up images so vivid they send you spinning off into reverie, or rivet you to your chair. Conversations full of subtle wit and running jokes and the *le mot juste*. It's just a very tricky horse to ride, and if you fall off it will trample you.

Neal Barrett can ride that horse in rings around anybody else. **The Hereafter Gang** is an instant classic, a modern western about sex, reincarnation, and soil immersion. The less I tell you about the plot the fewer surprises I'll ruin. Suffice to say it's about an ordinary early-middle-aged guy in Houston whose life suddenly gets strange, and then stranger, and then stranger still. What begins as an amorous escapade ends in a revelation about the inner workings of the universe; along the way we are treated to liberal doses of philosophy, nostalgia, vintage World War I *aeroplanes,* and car-hop sex. We even get to drink a beer with Jesus. Miss this one at your own risk. —Lewis Shiner

Monkey Brain Sushi

edited by Alfred Birnbaum

$9.95; Kodansha International
1991; 304 pp.

Americans are notorious for not reading books translated from other languages. For every commercially successful translation (such as Marquez's classic, **One Hundred Years of Solitude**, or Patrick Susskind's wonderfully perverse **Perfume**) dozens of other worthy books sit on store shelves until their covers are torn off and returned to the publisher for credit, and their pages are turned into Jiffy-Bag filler.

Here's your chance to break this pitiful cycle, educate and entertain yourself at the same time. **Monkey Brain Sushi** is a collection of 11 stories by some of Japan's most provocative contemporary writers. If, like some people, you're afraid you might not be able to relate to stories by modern Japanese writers writing for a modern Japanese audience, consider this: the forms of the stories in this anthology are as familiar as any you'll find at your local bookstore; **Monkey Brain Sushi** offers up science fiction, erotica, feminist lit and pomo/cut-ups/experimental lit. There's even a comic, looking back at the myths surrounding wartime Japan. Best of all, the translations themselves are bright and alive, not the kind of turgid afraid-to-interpret-the-work stuff they made you read in school. For any curious *gaijin*, **Monkey Brain Sushi** is a glimpse into a culture that is both as familiar as your daily life, and as different as *Kanji* ideograms and Roman letters.

The Touch

by Michael Brownstein
$7; Autonomedia
1993; 123 pp.

Author photos on books are meant to engage readers by showing how interesting or clever or attractive a writer is. They are a marketing device. Michael Brownstein's photo on the back of **The Touch** looks more like a mug shot than a literary invitation. Not an inappropriate opening image for this compact and dense narrative that examines the relationships between power and identity, memory and time, sex and the true enlightenment that comes when someone has passed through the heart of fire. Like many spiritual works, reading **The Touch** is itself a kind of rite of passage, but don't think for a moment that "spiritual" means "new agey" or "weak." This is a sort-of **Steppenwolf** as reworked by de Sade.

Fresh Carpet

by Ivor Cutler

1986; 60 pp.
information from: Noise Abatement Society, P.O. Box 8, Bromley,
Kent, BR2 0UM, England

This obscure little pink book crosses the genre of whimsical punk
rock lyric with the prose poem to create a collection of seventy-
eight tiny fantastical tales, with titles ranging from "Finger Flutter"
and "My Wee Pet" to "The Conservation of Matter" (about defecat-
ing on the moon) and "Feeble Try With a Stone." Dedicated to the
Noise Abatement Society, **Fresh Carpet** features illustrations by the
author (or should I say anti-illustrations: post-surrealist pencil
drawings which depict objects ironically related to each tale but
often not mentioned in the text).

Ivor Cutler has one of those offhand ways of turning the world
upside-down ("Hello stone. How are you?" "Well, I have a little pain
at the back...") Then he subtly turns it back right-side up again. Of
"Maturity" he writes "to combine public altruism with private self-
interest and unwitting hypocrisy is quite a trick, but I think I have it
now." Such idiosyncratic culture critique comes from the combined
sensibility of someone who has put out albums on Virgin
(**Dandruff**, **Velvet Donkey**, **Jammy Smears**) as well as a series of
children's books (**Herbert the Chicken**, **Herbert the Elephant**). In
his world, sounds can be soaked up with sponges, parrots hold
daddy-long-legs lunches to the sky "for a last look and to give them
a bit of flavour," and people put their ears to mountains "to hear
what a mountain sounded like." The top of a beloved's unwashed
hair gives rise to the intimate title "Dear Matting."

"Try clothing a thought with clear words to make it visible," he
writes. "Watch the awkward person struggle for the right word, the
honest word. Trust his integrity." And as Cutler himself might
respond to my review of his fanciful, surprising collection: "'Why
me?' I reply, determined to maintain the fiction of equality, voice
catching with egocentricity."—Miryam Sas

Rent Boy

by Gary Indiana

$14 ppd (NY residents add sales tax) from: High Risk Books, 401 W.
Broadway, NY, NY 10012; NY 800-283-3572; London 071-354-1949

The Rent Boy is for sale to anyone—man, woman, or whatever—with the cash to pay for his time. The Rent Boy is on the make in New York. He attends classes at Rutgers, hangs out, and when he's not hustling, holds down a straight job as a waiter and works hard at keeping his downtown too-hip-to-live veneer bright and sharp.

Like many such characters, the Rent Boy thinks he's got it all pretty much figured out. How the system works. If there's someone better than he at playing the game, the Rent Boy figures he'll work on his technique a little more, and he'll soon be the one on top. No problem. Then something happens...the Rent Boy fucks up. He gets too close to another Rent Boy—a weekend junk-user called Chip—who pulls the Rent Boy into a new scene, stranger than anything he's ever seen before. The doctor the Rent Boy meets through Chip isn't into sex like Chip's other friends. He's into organs. Human organs. Buying and selling. And he's got a very horny nurse who's developed a thing for the Rent Boy...

Rent Boy is a black *fin de siècle* sit-com, a drunken stroll through Manhattan's night life that ends in a three-way with Groucho Marx and Victor Frankenstein.

Avant-Pop: Fiction for a Daydream Nation

edited by Larry McCaffery
$7.00; Black Ice Books
1993; 247 pp.

Art-Lit and Pop-Cult Lit collide like excited particles in a cyclotron. What comes out the *other* end of the twisting magnetic text tube is something other. Words that won't stay still on the page, as hyperactive and jittery as video images, quick-cut and morphed into monsters and angels. This is the region where the novel might be dead, but words still carry a weight and power all their own.

The **Avant-Pop** anthology brings together such well-known language and fiction luminaries as Kathy Acker, Mark Leyner, Stephen Wright, Samuel Delany, William Vollman and Euridice with up-and-comers like Doug Rice, Tim Ferret, Derek Pell and Ricardo Cruz.

Fuck art, let's read.

Also recommended: **Across the Wounded Galaxies; Storming the Reality Studio**

The Torture Garden

by Octave Mirabeau

1989; 120 pp.; $17.99 ppd (foreign $19.99; CA residents add sales tax) from: RE/Search, 20 Romolo St., Ste. B, San Francisco, CA 94133

Every generation likes to think that it has the lock on the shocking and the extreme. Rap and punk shook up middle America with their combinations of fury, truth and violent fantasies. Before that there was Elvis. The Beats. Even Frank Sinatra was considered dangerous in the '40s. But to find real danger in pop culture, you have to go back to the very beginning of the century. Even before the Dadaists and the Surrealists were the Decadents of the *fin de siècle*, whose extravagant art gave depravity a bad name. It was one of this bunch, Octave Mirabeau, who wrote a novel that was referred to as "the most sickening work of the nineteenth century."

The Torture Garden is an exquisitely written story about a man bent on finding the limits of human experience, and his involvement with Clara, a powerful woman who guides him to a certain Chinese garden where torture is practiced as a form of art. What he finds there goes beyond anything he had ever imagined, both in awfulness and beauty. Readers will find that much modern horror pales in comparison to **The Torture Garden.**

The RE/Search edition is illustrated by Bobby Neel Adams' haunting photo illustrations; they capture both the mystery and beauty of the book's prose, and are a lovely piece of art all on their own.

A Wild Sheep Chase

by Haruki Murakami

$10.95, Plume Fiction
1989; 299 pp.

Haruki Murakami is 44 years old and his novels sell by the truckload in Tokyo. He's the voice of that large and raffish segment of the Japanese population who could give a rat's ass about careers or money, and vastly prefer to hang out in seedy coffee bars listening to old Chuck Berry records. A writer of extraordinary talent whose quiet voice and unique sense of atmosphere slowly spreads into the reader's mind like an oil stain.

A Wild Sheep Chase is the sequel to Murakami's **Pinball** (1973)

Our translator hero, now somewhat better-off financially than he was in the previous book, but as reckless as ever, becomes entangled with right-wing extremists, a sinister sheep with supernatural powers, and a girl with the most beautiful ears in the world. Japanese magic-realism with a kick like a five-legged mule.— Bruce Sterling

Also recommended: **Hard-Boiled Wonderland and the End of the World; The Elephant Vanishes; Dance Dance Dance; Norwegian Wood**

Tonguing the Zeitgeist

by Lance Olsen

1994; 192 pp.
$15 ppd (CA residents add sales tax) from: Permeable Press, 47 Noe St., #4, San Francisco, CA 94114

If **Tonguing the Zeitgeist** is any indication, living in the woods of the Pacific Northwest has brilliantly twisted Lance Olsen's mind. Riffing on established cyberpunk themes (isolation, hypertech, environmental destruction, conspiracy, overpopulation) but with a startling and distinctive writing voice, Olsen flings us down through the seven levels of Dystopia.

The Zeitgeist world's inventiveness and vivid solidity is matched neither by its characters' depth (an elusive, Proustian notion anyway) nor by originality of plot (it centers on rock & roll, which presents natural limitations). This might be part of the point, rather than just being an unfortunate side effect of sci-fi subject matter; the relationships between these folks evolve quickly, with tenuous bonds and uncertain intent. Our hero slaves away at the online equivalent of a phone farm (ya know, a mail order by phone sort of atmosphere) where he and his fellow microserfs concern themselves with the religion of pop-cult and whether they've properly applied their fake AIDS sores and Frankenstein neck-plugs today. There's a pop star who tunes in constantly to virtual reality scenarios of actual live violence taking place around the world while languidly masturbating, a corporate brown-nose in a Bauhaus dream-condo, and an impressive ensemble of the near-future's equivalents of classic junkies and whores.

Olsen manages to extend every excessive and decadent fad of our times—from body manipulation and techno-eroticism to the Cult of Aloneness—to its logical extreme without reveling in neophilia. The only condemnation which leaks through these action-paced, verb-cracking pages is against us, here and now. —Tiffany Lee Brown

Was

by Geoff Ryman
$10; Penguin
1992; 384 pp.

Geoff Ryman is a Canadian living in Britain. Naturally, his most recent novel is set in rural Kansas.

Was is a re-write, re-interpretation and re-digestion of **The Wizard of Oz,** as book, as movie and as cultural icon. **Was** details three lives each of which, in its own way, has been caught up in the Oz myth. Dorothy Gael is the sad and lonely young farm girl who lives with her aunt and uncle in the landlocked plains of Kansas; young Judy Garland is the actress who would later play a fantasy version of Dorothy's life in the movies, acting out the happy childhood each of them had missed. Years later Jonathan, an actor dying of AIDS, travels to Kansas to investigate the life of the real Dorothy Gael—now long dead—whose life never took her to Oz, but to an asylum.

In **Was,** Ryman does a fast fade between fantasy and reality, slipping between the lives of real and imagined people, proving that all lives are imagined in the end—some tragically, some heroically. This is the story of lives and the story of a story, and how a children's tale can entangle the lives of so many people.

Also recommended: **Unconquered Countries; The Warrior Who Carried Life; The Child Garden**

Girlfriend Number One

Lesbian Life in the 90s
Edited by Robin Stevens
$12.95; Cleis Press
1994: 222 pp.

What constitutes a lesbian date? Hell if I could tell you (even though I'd been out on a few) until I read **Girlfriend Number One.** This is a compilation of writing by women who've performed at San Francisco's famous Red Dora's Bearded Lady Cafe (where even the femmes are butch). None of these women are famous, they're just everyday grrrls reporting on what it's like to be a dyke—especially a dyke in a small community of like-minded dykes.

These women poke fun at themselves and their community with

jokes (Question: "What does a lesbian bring on the second date?" Answer: "A U-Haul.") and the morbid fascination lesbians have with "processing issues."

One definition of a lesbian date is "something that inspires poetry." In the case of this book, lesbian dates seemed to have inspired insight, pride, and horniness. If you're a dyke, you'll probably see yourself reflected somewhere on these pages, but you only need to be a little queer to understand the anger, vulnerability and mirth that these women are expressing.—Daryl-Lynn Johnson

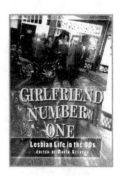

Technosex

edited by Cecilia Tan

1993; 84 pp.
$9.20 ppd (MA residents add sales tax) from: Circlet Press, P.O. Box 15143, Boston, MA 02215

You can't talk about new tech without also acknowledging two fast-moving groups who are likely to be way ahead of the curve on all kinds of personal electronics: criminals and the sexual underground. Both groups are, in a real sense, explorers. Criminals, however, have a fairly simple goal in mind as they venture into uncharted gizmo territory: they want to separate you from your money. The explorations of the sexual underground, however, are more internal and, so, harder to map. We can say, though, that sexual explorers use technology to experience power and submission, pleasure and pain, in new and unexpected ways—just look at how many ways people have found to use vibrating "neck massagers." So what will the sexual cosmonauts, computer jockeys and carnal prospectors do when home-based virtual reality systems become common? Or robots? Or Artificial Intelligence systems? Who will be the first people to fuck in Zero-G?

These last few questions are explored by the authors of the seven erotically charged stories in **Technosex,** from Circlet Press. Circlet has carved out its own territory in erotic publishing with anthologies that mix fantasy and science fiction with hardcore erotic writing. Some of their other noteworthy titles are **Telepaths Don't Need Safewords, SexMagick (Women Conjuring Erotic Fantasy)** and **Worlds of Women (Sapphic Science Fiction Erotica).**

Uncle Ovid's Exercise Book

by Don Webb

1988; 154 pp.
information from: Mark V. Ziesing, P.O. Box 76, Shingletown, CA 96088; 916-474-1580

Both a parody and homage to Ovid's poetic story cycle, **Metamorphosis,** Don Webb's version of that work of fantastic mini-fictions contains at least 97 different reasons (i.e., stories) to read this book.

Take Metamorphosis No. 45: we start out with a little lecture and rumination on William Burroughs' famous line, "Language is a virus from outer space," and end with the tale of a poor guy doing a Cronenbergesque transformation into a piece of extraterrestrial punctuation. Then there's Metamorphosis No. 67, in which the book, **Uncle Ovid's Exercise Book,** begins to turn into the diary of a mysterious Mrs. Brandon. Or Metamorphosis No. 2, which links self-improvement courses, Grimm Brothers' fairy tales and certain types of effervescent stomach gas medications. And there are 94 other tiny stories, theories, bon-mots and sleight-of-hand tricks.

Uncle Ovid's Exercise Book is one of the real treasures of the small press world.

Dogs in Lingerie

by Danielle Willis

1990; 75 pp.
$6.95 ppd (CA residents add sales tax) from: Zeitgeist Press, 4368 Piedmont Ave., Oakland, CA 94611

Danielle Willis is a sex worker, writer, and performance artist. **Dogs in Lingerie** is her collection of prose poems depicting both the sex biz and Willis' dark obsessions in a sharp mixture of cinema-verité and Goth Romanticism. The perspective here is from the world of the stripper and the prostitute, the last being a position so outside accepted society that when a hooker is killed the police often don't even bother to investigate, labeling the case *NHI:* No Human Involvement.

Through Willis' words, the world of the sex worker melts between the consuming and alluring decadence of "The Methedrine Dollhouse" ("...and you take a drag off/ one of your Dunhills/ and tell the guy on the/ phone you're much too/ exhausted to tie him up/ so he'll just have to/ content himself with/ sucking you off instead/ your spine is showing like/ a ridge of fingertips/ through your night-gown/ and last night I dreamed/ we rode on the backs of manta rays through/ gardens of the drowned/ where ghosts with eyes/ like comb jellies murmur/ over the bones of pirates...") and the harsh grind of "Dogs in Lingerie" ("...the usual afternoon/ porno crowd was there,/ about fifteen docile/ older guys slumped in/ their chairs like/ lobot-omy patients/ clutching flyers with/ a picture of a Doberman pinsch-er/in a black rubber dress/ beneath the legend/ BITCHES IN HEAT...").

Dogs in Lingerie is powerful stuff. By turns autobiography, reportage and fantasy, all corseted in a poetry that smacks you with the strength and attention-demanding reality of a riding crop across the small of your back.

Through the Arc of the Rain Forest

by Karen Tei Yamashita
$9.95; Coffee House Press
1990; 212 pp.

For those who prefer some classification, **Through the Arc of the Rain Forest** is poetic satire. Yamashita successfully sustains a care-fully woven interdependent network of fantastic themes in a pro-found black comedy. Her treatment of the cast of bizarre but all-too-human characters is warm and sympathetic. Caught up in a mad whirlwind of synchronicities, eccentricities, technological idealism and blind faith, a three-armed American CEO, a Japanese man with a strange sphere floating six inches in front of his head, a French ornithologist with three breasts, and a naive and simple peasant who discovers the art of healing by tickling the ear with feathers all achieve fame and fortune on a mysterious polymer plain called the Matacão that has emerged in the rain forest. In this accelerating montage, Yamashita plays out an unforgettable soap opera of the boom and bust of Western civilization and its abstract, plastic cul-ture which ends in the destruction of Brazilian Amazonia and all the birds of paradise.

This is an entertaining read full of twists and turns, magic and poignant logic which never fails to connect.—David Memmott

Also recommended: **Brazil Maru**

Xuxa

by Amelia Simpson

$14.95; Temple University Press
1993; 238 pp.

Xuxa is like a character from a porn movie written by Baudrillard and directed by McLuhan. Her most accessible face is as the host of a phenomenally successful Brazil-based kids' show. But even in that simple image are contradictions: Xuxa's kiddie show is a construct as well-planned and ordered as neurosurgery, a bright and rapid-fire combination of songs, games and teasing sexuality. Xuxa herself plays hostess in hot pants and tiny tops. She is surrounded by equally leggy teenage nymphets, *paquitas*, who keep the show moving and the kids in line. As a media package, Xuxa is almost perfect. Her combination of sexy moves and maternal images continues to short-circuit both the dullness of kiddie show safety and complaints about her erotic persona. She's Mommy and Temptress in one buns-of-steel-Aryan-wetdream package, as popular with Dads as she is with the children. And the ever-present *paquitas* complete the picture, giving the little girls in the audience something to aspire to and the boys something to fantasize about.

Xuxa, future kiddie show mega-star, at age 19, Rio de Janeiro, 1982. Photo courtesy of AP/Wide World Photos.

It's no accident that Xuxa's star first rose in Brazil, a developing country notorious for watching more TV than any other nation in the region. Xuxa is a product of TV marketing, moving through the video screen into viewers' homes and weaving herself into every aspect of daily life, a consumer icon.

Her face graces not only her show, and her own magazine, modeling school, travel agency, limo service and line of clothing stores, but alsobikes, yogurt, surfboards, shampoo, cosmetics, soup...She's the first Latin American entertainer to ever make the *Forbes* list of big money stars. What does her fame tell us about Brazilian culture, and by extension the image-hungry and well-wired first world?

Amelia Simpson looks at Xuxa's career, from her early days as a *Playboy* model and soft-core porn actress to her more recent successes. Simpson's main focus is on Xuxa as both media construct and marketing device, and dissects the star's selling of "gender, race and modernity." And if we in North America think it's quaint that Latin America has opted for a blonde and smiling Big Brother surrogate, all we have to do is think back to the thorough and precisely orchestrated media manipulation by the Reagan administration's "Morning in America" period and Gulf War boosterism to see that we aren't immune to media images that reinforce our dreams of who we wish ourselves to be.

Secret Journal

1836-1837

by A. S. Pushkin

1991; 91 pp.
$21 ppd ($25 foreign) from: M.I.P. Co., P.O. Box 27484, Minneapolis, MN 55427; fax 612-544-6077

Aleksandr Sergeyevich Pushkin is revered in Russia as the founder of their modern poetry, and for introducing vernacular speech into literature. During the years he was writing his major works, however, he was also keeping a secret diary. It's also well-known that Pushkin was killed in a duel. Now we know why.

A. S. Pushkin, Russian literary saint who wove everyday speech, myth, and history into his work, was fucking pretty much any babe who would hold still. Starting with his wife and her two sisters, Pushkin continues in his quest for fresh flesh throughout the tonier parlors of nineteenth-century Moscow, writing like a cross between a high romantic and Hugh Hefner at his most adolescent. "Each time I get a hard-on," writes Pushkin, "it means that my cock is turned to Heaven and to God. And whenever it is hard, I know that God is with me." And, "I am unable to say no to a woman. At least I fuck her out of courtesy. Indeed, my heart belongs to the easiest woman."

For the Russian literary world, this book is a bit of a shock. Imagine telling Americans you found Washington's diary and discovered that he crossed the Delaware River because he heard that on the other side was a great little hooker who gave head like a rabid mongoose.

Bad Girls Do It!

An Encyclopedia of Female Murderers
by Michael Newton

1993; 205 pp.
$18.95 ppd (WA residents add sales tax) from: Loompanics
Unlimited, P.O. Box 1197, Port Townsend, WA 98368

Sisters are doing it for themselves and, according to **Bad Girls Do It!**, have been doing it for some time. Serial murder, that is. Although we don't generally think of female criminals in terms of murder (most women doing time are in for non-violent offenses such as prostitution, fraud and embezzlement), there have been plenty of female killers. Erzsebet (Elizabeth) Bathory is among the earliest and bloodiest of the murderers chronicled in **Bad Girls Do It!**. In the sixteenth century, Bathory became a kind of female Gilles de Rais, buying or kidnapping young women from the nearby villages and torturing them to death. By the time the crown got fed up with her little hobby, she'd done in between 300 and 650 local women.

Bad Girls Do It! profiles 182 female multiple murderers up to, and including, Aileen Wournos, the Florida prostitute convicted of icing six unruly johns. As the book says, "**Bad Girls Do It!** proves that the urge to kill is an equal opportunity affliction."

The Motion of Light in Water

Sex and Science Fiction Writing in the East Village
by Samuel R. Delany

$12.95; Masquerade Books
1993; 520 pp.

Samuel Delany is one of the most influential science fiction writers alive; his works inspired both the first wave of cyberpunks and introduced a messy, ambivalent sexuality to a genre that is slowly growing out of its adolescent groping phase. **The Motion of Light in Water** is at times an experiment in memory and language, a compelling portrait of New York in the '60s, and an unusually open and sexually honest autobiography by one of the few writers whose life has been interesting enough to warrant having it in print. This new edition is also the first time the unexpurgated version has been available from a U.S. publisher.

- *Ana was dark-haired, full-bodied, very smart, very talented, and she lived with an older man (thirty-five or so, ahem) named Fred, who used to come to the coffee shops where she performed and, gazing through his wire-framed glasses, waited for her sets to be finished with, then would walk with her, carrying her guitar case, back to the Second Avenue apartment (hers) they shared. For a while, both Marilyn and I alternated between being flattered and being a bit annoyed by her attentions. I guess one evening, when she was over visiting us, to sing for us a song or three she had just written, we both decided to be flattered at the same time. The three of us ended up in bed together.*

  For me it was an abundance of breasts; a thicket of thighs; an arbor of arms. There was a lot of laughing, a lot of quiet affection, and mouths moved everywhere over the various hills of various bodies. I was fascinated to see that a certain politics of attention applied here, prone, with two women I knew as friends just as much as it did, over at the trucks, upright, with four men who were complete strangers.

  Because feelings, emotional and physical, are so foregrounded in sexual encounters, the orgy is the most social of human interchanges, where awareness and communication, whether verbal or no, hold all together or sunder it.

Difficult Lives

Jim Thompson—David Goodis—Chester Himes
by James Sallis
1993; 99 pp.
$12 ppd from: Gryphon Publications, P.O. Box 209, Brooklyn, NY 11228-0209

A brief, but riveting look at the crime novel and the lives and works of three of America's best genre novelists: Jim Thompson, the alcoholic "dime-store Dostoevski;" David Goodis, the neurotic and eccentric rags-to-riches-to-rags-and-his-mother's-sofa kid; and Chester Himes, who wrote about urban black life in a style that slipped easily between street journalism and Book of Revelations-scale apocalyptic imagery.

Difficult Lives author, James Sallis, is no slouch himself in the fiction department. He's written two excellent mysteries, **The Long-Legged Fly** and **Moth,** and is the author of some excellent short stories, many of which you can find in Damon Knight's **Orbit** science fiction series in used bookstores.

Bodies and Machines

by Mark Seltzer
$15.95; Routledge
1992; 236 pp.

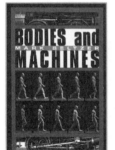

"Nothing typifies the American sense of identity more than the love of nature (nature's nation) except perhaps the love of technology (made in America)," says author Mark Seltzer.

There is probably an unavoidable psychological link between humans and the machines they produce. Inevitably, one comes to be judged by the other. Since machines are simpler in their operation and goals, there is a natural inclination to compare the more complex (and sometimes incomprehensible) human system to the machine. It's the very nature of human complexity that has led many writers and theorists to see the relatively simple and knowable characteristics of the machine as something humans should aspire to.

This attitude pervaded culture— from the popular world to the academics—for over a century, and was particularly strong in the opening years of the 20th century. The idea of machine "standardization" became so popular, in fact, that it was used as a basis to train workers on how to move and use their bodies in a more efficient, i.e. machine-like, manner. It also popularized sciences such as eugenics. When ideas such as standardization and eugenics combine, you often end up with cultural writs on the ideal human form. And as anyone who has looked at the models in any popular magazine can tell you, that process still

The Composite Photograph, or Pictorial Statistics

goes on, subtly, today.

By looking at a range of scholarly and popular "naturalist" documents that range from the 1850s to the 1920s, Seltzer "traces the remaking of nature in terms of the *naturalist machine* and the remaking of individuals as statistical *persons.*"

- *The merger between the desire to quantify and the desire to see makes possible, for example, the visual display of persons in the form of what eugenicist Francis Galton called composite photographs or "pictorial statistics"...(which an 1894 article describes as) "employing the photographic camera to combine the features of a number of individuals upon the same sensitive plate, thus producing a typical portrait of the group by (as Galton puts it) 'bringing into evidence'" all common traits "and leaving 'but a ghost of a trace of individual peculiarities.'" The composite photograph provided the necessary visual analog of a social typology and of deviations from type, merging looking and measuring in a standard, and standardizing, schema.*

The Human Body Shop

The Engineering and Marketing of Life
by Andrew Kimbrell
$22; HarperCollins
1993; 348 pp.

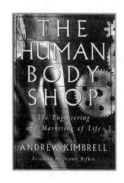

The marketing department has invaded the biotech lab, and they're making big bucks for everyone involved. From transgenic mice (rodents whose immune systems have been genetically snipped out) to the international human organ gray market, there's never been a higher interest in what makes humans tick, and how much someone would be willing to pay for a shot of it. And who's regulating this exploding new industry? Well, various groups and offices stick their toes in the regulatory water, but no one really wants to go for a swim. And with the on-going Human Genome Project, chances are by the time those researchers finish mapping our entire genetic code, we'll have the information to patent life—meaning you and me—down to our DNA. And then what? Who owns that information, that genetic material?

The zone where biotech and commerce meet isn't a pretty place, filled as it is with the shadows of real and potential monsters, but it's a place you can't afford to ignore. **The Human Body Shop** is a tour guide to this fascinating and, sometimes, grotesque world.

Femalia

edited by Joani Blank

1993; 72 pp.
$18 ppd (CA residents add sales tax) from: Down There Press, 938 Howard St., San Francisco, CA 94103

The one unquestionable difference between men and women is the orientation of their genitals to their bodies, i.e., men are mostly "outies," while women are primarily "innies." Because vulvas are mostly hidden from view—and easy inspection—women frequently grow up believing, as **Femalia** editor, Joani Blank, puts it, "that in one way or another, their genitals are not quite 'normal.' "

This book should remedy some of those fears. Consisting simply of a short introduction, a diagram and 32 full-color photos of women's vulvas, **Femalia** demonstrates that like faces, personalities and whole bodies, there are an infinite number of variations when it comes to the color, shape and size of individual genitals.

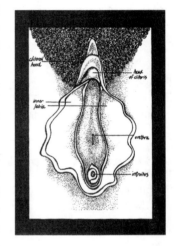

A helpful diagram of the vulva from Femalia.

Whether you find this book beautiful or arousing (or, I suppose, the work of Satan's minions) will be determined by your individual tastes. If, however, you don't find **Femalia** to be a lovely bit of body art, you'll probably find it instructive in the many variations possible in the expression of human skin and tissue.

The Last Sex

Feminism and Outlaw Bodies
edited by Arthur & Marilouise Kroker
$15.95; St. Martin's Press
1993; 249 pp.

Ever since the Industrial Revolution proved that you could mechanize activities that previously had been people-powered, the human body has been in a constant state of identity crisis. The refinements and subtleties of the digital age have only made this anxiety of flesh all the more acute. But the bump and grind of science doesn't stop at the frame of a Jacquard loom or a computer terminal. We've learned to surgically alter our bodies in ways as profound as the way the machine revolution altered work.

The Last Sex is an anthology that looks at the future of gender in an age when the transgendered have emerged as a walking and breathing challenge to old sex definitions. "Should gender be our most fundamental distinction?" the editors ask. "Or is gender just another cult as described by (male-to-female transsexual) Kate Bornstein in this volume, or something even more insidious? Is gender a deadly virus?"

Both the editors and the authors in **The Last Sex** (including Kathy Acker, Shannon Bell, Kate Bornstein and Stephen Pfohl) challenge many basic assumptions about our roles and bodies in a gendered world. The book is, in effect, a rallying cry for what the editors call "transgenic gender," a new gender that lies outside of the dualistic man/woman model: an in-between gender, free of all the old cultural baggage, that might lead the way "into an aesthetic of sexual play."

At the end of the 20th century, we can no longer take the form of the human body for granted. The morphed body is the body of the future. Like an updated **Gray's Anatomy** for this emerging body, **The Last Sex** will speed your journey through this new, human-made adolescence.

- *Kate Bornstein: I know why transgendered and transsexual people aren't included (in the gay movement). It gets back to passing—you have to be a man, you have to be a woman. But my existence within a lesbian and gay community is threatening to the very foundations of that community. Here I am. I am saying that I'm not a man and I'm not a woman. So what happens when a lesbian is attracted to me? I call into question her lesbian identity.*

  It is a problem for anyone whose identity is wrapped up in a bipolar gender system. It is fascinating that we would pin all of our sexual orientation on the gender of sexual partners rather than a person's age or the sexual activity—what the person does in sex. This is why I really like the SM world. People into SM are pinning their sexual orientation on what they do and not who they do it with, necessarily. This is a tidal wave, about to crash.

The Gemstone File

edited by Jim Keith

1992; 214 pp.
$17.95 ppd (NY residents add sales tax) from: Sky Books, P.O. Box 769, Westbury, NY 11590

The Gemstone File is sort of the unified field theory of the conspiracy world. Covering events from 1932 to 1975, the documents that make up the book **The Gemstone File** bring together Aristotle Onassis, the Kennedy Assassination, Chappaquiddick, the Vietnam war, the Mob, Howard Hughes, Nixon, J. Edgar Hoover, dope smugglers, the CIA, the Vatican, Daniel Ellsberg, the Star Wars missile system...and on and on.

The files themselves are supposed to have been written by Bruce Roberts, copied and circulated hand-to-hand around the world for years. As one of the authors admits in one of the dozen appendices to the file, there's no way of knowing if most of this is true. **The Gemstone File** is, however, weirdly provocative and entertaining and, if you're a believer in unseen forces conspiring to shape politics and nations, this book is a feast.

The Secret History of the New World Order

by Herbert G. Dorsey III

1992; 81 pp.
$10 ppd ($11 foreign)

The Secret Space Program

by Herbert G. Dorsey III

1992; 71 pp.
$10 ppd ($11 foreign) both from: The Secret Information Network, P.O. Box 3185, W. Sedona, AZ 86340

The Illuminati and international banking are the twin poles of power in the world according to the small press, no-frills tome, **The Secret History of the New World Order.** Part of a 200-year, globe-spanning plan, the Illuminati/Bank cartel has engineered both of our previous World Wars and has plans for another, centered in the Middle East. They put Clinton in the White House and also plan to combine the Russian and U.S. armed forces into a single world cop force which they, of course, would control.

Essentially a condensation from numerous other books and first-hand sources, **The Secret History of the New World Order** is brisk and compelling reading.

By the same author is **The Secret Space Program,** a report on a massive cover-up of U.S. space technology advances obtained from crashed saucers discovered by American and German scientists. Information includes the existence of the U.S.'s anti-gravity ships and secret moonbases, as well as Eisenhower's 1954 treaty with aliens from the star system Betelgeuse.

Both books come with extensive bibliographies.

Casebook on Alternative 3

UFOs, Secret Societies and World Control
by Jim Keith
$12.95; IllumiNet Press
1994; 160 pp.

From Geneva, the Powers That Be—who control the wealth and power of the world's nations and corporations—are running their own space program. Working together secretly, the U.S. and Russia have set up bases on the moon and Mars using spacecraft that have far more power than anything the public knows about (these are the same crafts that account for most reported UFO sightings). Both scientists and ordinary citizens are being "disappeared" all over the world as part of the secret space program. The scientists run the off-world bases, while the people pulled off the street work at forced labor to keep the bases running. Why does this secret space program exist? So that the power elite of the planet earth can escape the coming environmental and population catastrophe they helped to create!

Even Jim Keith, the author of **Casebook on Alternative 3**, admits that the above scenario is hard to swallow. But, aside from the book references, press reports, and anecdotal evidence he supplies, Keith makes a simple and compelling argument for the scenario to be possible. "I would have to agree with *Alternative 3* that the rats who so lavishly profit from a foundering Spaceship Earth can be counted on to desert it..."

Secret and Suppressed

Banned Ideas & Hidden History
edited by Jim Keith

$12.95; Feral House
1993; 309 pp.

This book brings together ideas and alternate takes on history that challenge many accepted versions of "truth" and "reality." Are the Freemasons the secret power behind the British monarchy and so committed the Jack-the-Ripper murders to get rid of a talkative prostitute? Did a hapless patient in Sweden have an experimental electromagnetic transmitter implanted in his skull as part of a CIA experiment? Is AIDS a Pentagon germ warfare project that worked a little too well? Was a health reporter at an L.A. television station a clone produced by the government working with aliens? Did Jim Morrison's father collaborate with U.S. Intelligence agencies to unleash numerous fake-Morrisons for espionage work?

Pravda **cartoon showing U.S. scientist and military officer exchanging a vial of AIDS virus for money.**

Secret and Suppressed contains articles, rants, photos and more provocative questions and answers than a dozen other similar books.

The Montauk Project

Experiments in Time
by Preston B. Nichols with Peter Moon

1992; 160 pp.
$18.95 ppd (NY residents add sales tax) from: Sky Books, P.O. Box 769, Westbury, NY 11590

According to several accounts of the "Philadelphia Experiment," in 1943 U.S. Naval Research was trying to find a way to make its ships invisible to enemy radar. What they ended up doing was not only making a destroyer escort, the *USS Eldridge*, invisible, but also sending the thing through a rift in time.

According to author Preston B. Nichols, the time experiments continued for 40 years after the Philadelphia incident, ending at the Montauk Point, Long Island, Air Force Base. More than that, during his initial investigation, Nichols became convinced that he had taken part in the experiments, and then was conditioned to forget them.

This is Nichols' first-hand account of the time travel experiments conducted in Long Island. The book incorporates accounts of both time travel and brainwashing (to forget things and as part of a Manchurian Candidate-type plot), and also telepathy, travel to the interior of Martian pyramids, and the electromagnetic transference of a soul from one body to another.

For those with continuing interest, Sky Books also has a quarterly newsletter, *The Montauk Pulse* ($12/year), and a video of the base itself, *The Montauk Tour Video* ($42.95 ppd).

- *The (time) tunnel resembled a corkscrew with an effect similar to lit bulbs. It was a fluted sort of structure and not a straight tunnel. It twisted and took turns until you'd come out the other end. There, you would meet somebody or do something, you would complete your mission and return. The tunnel would open for you, and you'd come back to where you came from. However, if they lost power during the operation, you'd be lost in time or abandoned somewhere in the vortex itself. When someone was lost, it was usually caused by a glitch in hyperspace. And although many were lost, the scientists didn't abandon people deliberately or carelessly....*

  It was routine to create a tunnel, grab somebody off the street and send them down. Most of the time these people were winos or derelicts whose absence wouldn't create a furor. If they returned, they would make a full report on what they had encountered. Most of the winos used for the experiments were sobered up for a week before entering a portal, but many didn't make it back. We don't know how many people are still floating around in time, whenever, wherever, and however.

Final Exit

The Practicalities of Self-Deliverance and Assisted Suicide for the Dying

by Derek Humphry

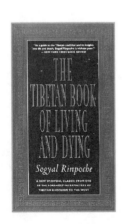

1991; 192 pp.
$18 ppd from: The National Hemlock Society, P.O. Box 11830, Eugene, OR 97440-3900; 503-342-5748

A responsible how-to suicide guide for terminally ill adults. It also has important information for potential helpers, or those who simply want to support a loved one's decision. There are specific drug recommendations, as well as dosage and administration techniques. **Final Exit** also has information for doctors and nurses on ways to handle a patient's request for euthanasia.

The author, Derek Humphry, is a journalist and past-president of the World Federation of Right to Die Societies. In 1980 he launched the Hemlock Society, a group dedicated to providing information on suicide and hospice alternatives to the terminally ill, and to lobbying for Right to Die legislation in California. You can get membership information from the address above.

The Tibetan Book of Living and Dying

by Sogyal Rinpoche
$14.00; HarperCollins
1993; 425 pp.

The Tibetan Book of the Dead is a handbook for a good death and a good entry into the afterlife. It speaks specifically about the process of death and the rituals, tests, and entities that a spirit will meet after it leaves the body. The idea of a training manual for death may seem strange to Western minds, but Tibetan Buddhist teachers weave the inevitability of death into daily thought and ritual so that their followers can live a fuller life and, according to Sogyal Rinpoche, so that they "are not condemned to go out empty-handed at death to meet the unknown."

The Tibetan Book of Living and Dying is Sogyal Rinpoche's rewrite and reinterpretation of **The Tibetan Book of the Dead** for a modern Western audience. It manages to cover both esoteric

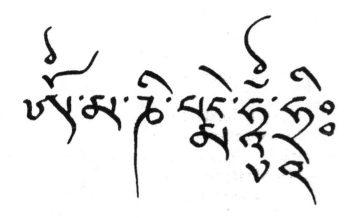

The Buddhist Mantra of Compassion, OM MANI PADME HUM, embodies the compassion and blessing of all the Buddhas and Bodhisattvas.

Buddhist teachings for those who want them, and also contains much practical advice on everyday life. Why should you be interested in a handbook on what sounds like a depressing subject? As Sogyal says in his introduction, "What more chilling commentary on the modern world could there be than that most people die unprepared for death, as they have lived, unprepared for life?"

• SAYING GOODBYE

It is not only the tensions that you have to learn to let go of, but the dying person as well. If you are attached and cling to the dying person, you can bring him or her a lot of unnecessary heartache and make it very hard for the person to let go and die peacefully....When people ask me how best to give someone permission to die, I tell them to imagine themselves standing by the bedside of the person they love and saying with the deepest and most sincere tenderness: "I am here with you and I love you. You are dying, and that is completely natural; it happens to everyone. I wish you could stay here with me, but I don't want you to suffer any more. The time we have had together has been enough, and I shall always cherish it. Please now don't hold onto life any longer. Let go. I give you my full and heartfelt permission to die. You are not alone, now or ever. You have all my love."

Encyclopedia of Death

by Robert & Beatrice Kastenbaum
$15; Avon Books
1989; 295 pp.

From definitions of mundanities like "Death Certificate" and "Autopsy" to death-related exotica, such as Melanesian funeral services and cryonic suspension, the **Encyclopedia of Death** is one-stopping shopping for death-data.

For instance, did you know that traditional lullabies from around the world often contain images of death and violence? Finland, in particular, is home to such sweet-dream songs as *Rock the Child to Tuonela* (the land of death). Did you know that besides *rigor mortis* (stiffening of the joints because of involuntary muscle contractions after death), there is also *algor mortis* (the fall in body temperature after death; approximately two degrees an hour, until the body reaches room temperature) and *livor mortis* (the skin discoloration that occurs when red blood cells start to break down). Did you know that the most common type of cryonic suspension (freezing the terminally ill just before death) is "neurosuspension," which only preserves the head? Well, now you do. And you can learn a lot more fun facts about passing on in the **Encyclopedia of Death**.

Cryonic suspension storage units as used by the Alcor Life Extension Foundation. The large unit (9' tall) stores one or two complete bodies. The smaller unit below is for neurosuspension (head-only preservation) and can hold from one to four heads. Used by permission of Alcor Life Extension Foundation, 12327 Doherty St., Riverside, CA 92503; 714-736-1703.

The Forbidden Zone

by Michael Lesy
$7.95; Anchor Books
1987; 250 pp.

Most of us are so separated from death in our daily lives that we don't want to talk about it, think about it, or hear about it. But what about those people who bunk with death every night? How do they deal with it? In **The Forbidden Zone** Michael Lesy takes us on a walking tour of people in the near-death biz: pathologists, homicide detectives, slaughterhouse workers (both secular and Orthodox Jewish shochets), undertakers, guys who work on a prison's Death Row, a mercenary, and AIDS patients and their doctors.

As you might expect, **The Forbidden Zone** has its share of moments both beautiful and awful, touching and surreal. What makes the book work, in the end, is Lesy, the author. He's no straight-news journalist, but a writer of real sensitivity who is alternately touched, fascinated and appalled by his subject matter and the people he meets. By sharing his personal reactions—his doubts, fears and occasional moments of illumination—with the reader, Lesy has created a remarkable book about a subject that many people regard only with horror.

Also recommended: **Wisconsin Death Trip**

- *Raymond (the embalmer): "What you need is a nice firm base for your makeup. Restoration's something else again. I worked ten hours on one fella, once. He'd gone into the back of a truck in a Volkswagen at fifty miles an hour. Automobile accidents are always like that: a lot of head and face work. You gotta join the fractures and fill in with your plaster of Paris; suture the cuts and seal 'em with your suture seal and your drying powder; fill in the cracks and build 'em up with your wax, then smooth it all down and do your cosmetizing. The only trouble was, I must not have used enough suture seal, 'cause when we lifted him up and put him in the casket, one side of his face fell off. There musta been fluid under the wax, so when we moved him, it cracked and the whole thing slid off. Took me five more hours to get him right."*

The Art and Science of Embalming

by A. O. Spriggs

1971; 312 pp.
information from: Discount Medical Books, 345 Judah St., San Francisco, CA 94122; 415-664-5555; fax 415-664-7810

The title pretty much says it all. This is a straight instructional text covering everything from basic anatomy to blood-draining techniques to reattaching a severed head to a body. The interior illustrations range from restrained Victoriana to simple line drawings, so if you're looking for cool pictures of dead people, you'll just have to fall back on your diseased imagination.

Culture Jamming

Culture Jamming, Hacking, Slashing and Sniping
in the Empire of Signs
by Mark Dery

1993; 17 pp.
$8 ppd (foreign $9) from: Open Magazine Pamphlet Series, P.O.
Box 2726, Westfield, NJ 07091; 908-789-9608

Just as Duchamp drew a mustache on a copy of the Mona Lisa to say goodbye to old ideas about art, so the information age demands a new breed of artist who can tape a KICK ME sign to the back of the contemporary communications web. Mark Dery's profile of this new type of artist—billboard modifiers, zine publishers, hackers, subvertisers, media pranksters—shows them walking a fine line between "terrorist" and "aesthete," creating by reinterpreting, transforming and redistributing the storm of data that defines and surrounds our daily lives. **Culture Jamming** isn't about art that hangs on gallery walls, but art that gets under your skin: a cultural calamine lotion; it doesn't destroy the poison that causes the itch, but it eases the pain so that you can think again.

Textual Poachers

Television Fans & Participatory Culture
by Henry Jenkins
$16.95; Routledge
1992; 343 pp.

Everyone who's published their writing, broadcast their words or played their music for an audience knows that you cannot control other people's reactions or interpretations of your work. That's important: What you say may not be the message that comes across. This situation is especially true in the case of television, a visual medium, where the words and images may clash, or they may reinforce each other in unintended ways. **Star Trek** is a good example of this phenomenon.

In **Textual Poachers,** author Henry Jenkins writes about a subgroup of fandom obsessed with Kirk/Spock pornography and erotica. Where does this idea come from? Clearly, while the basic text of **Star Trek** was relentlessly heterosexual, enough diehard fans read into it a subtext of homoerotic lust that the producers never consciously intended. And **Star Trek** isn't the only television to have inspired fan erotica. **The Man From U.N.C.L.E., Starsky and Hutch, Beauty and the Beast,** and **Blake's 7** all have their own underground networks of fan pornographers and obsessives.

What does this mean? Is it just another example of people who should get a life? Not necessarily. According to Jenkins, these fans already have quite rich lives, albeit often fantasy-inspired, built around appropriating the media images they love and rewriting them for the parts of their own lives that extend beyond the television screen. **Textual Poachers** examines the ways these fans are reversing the traditional process of mass media, which appropriates iconic images and sells them back to us in a pre-packaged form. These fans are reappropriating those images and creating a new, text- and art-based network that more fully represents the scope of their desires.

"Intimacy, Trust and Fairness": The Man from U.N.C.L.E.'s Napoleon Solo and Ilya Kuryakin. Art work by Suzan Lovett

- *"Welcome to bisexuality, Captain Kirk, where gender has nothing to do with who you want."*

  Thus begins Gayle Feyrer's The Cosmic Fuck series, a vintage example of Kirk/Spock fan erotica, a story exploring what is for the story's protagonists a "strange new world"—the realm of bisexuality and its unsanctioned pleasures. As the series continues, Kirk works through his initial discomfort and anxiety, learns to adjust to these unfamiliar sensations, comes to accept his own break with the regimentation of sexual orientation; Spock learns to be more open about his feelings, moves beyond the chemical analysis of Kirk's sperm ("fascinating, Captain") to a more spontaneous expression of his affections. The men's love grows and their consciousness expands through the magic of the mind meld. In the end, their love is so firm it can be broadened further, incorporating McCoy in a friendly menage a trois that mirrors the familiar gathering of three buddies that concludes many of the broadcast episodes.

Radiotext(e)

edited by Neil Strauss with David Mandl

$12; Semiotext(e)/Autonomedia
1994; 352 pp.

If you think television is a strange device, it's got nothing on radio. **Radiotext(e)** is a centenary collection of essays on radio broadcasting and contains such practical information as how to build radio transmitters and break into commercial broadcasting. The real jewels in this collection, though, are the essays that rip off the secret, bizarre, and insidious uses people have made of wireless transmit-

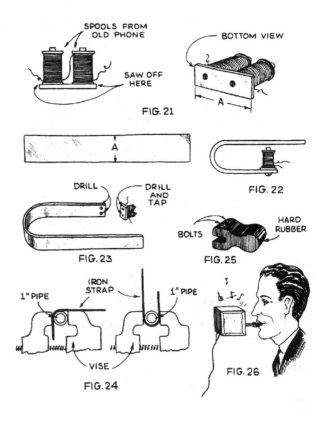

Technical diagram for a device that let you hear radio through your teeth.

ters. UFO hunters and astronomers routinely use radio to scan the sky for space visitors and pulsars, respectively. Others radio pioneers have used the box to contact the dead, tap into telepathic transmissions, project their own thoughts into others' heads, and broadcast programs through listeners' teeth.

The straight side of radio is here, too: Transcripts of Edward R. Murrow's first-person description of the Buchenwald concentration camp and Emperor Hirohito's broadcast officially announcing the surrender of Japan in WWII. Some of the other writers included include George Orwell, La Monte Young, Hakim Bey, Bertolt Brecht, Kurt Schwitters and Ezra Pound.

Happy 100th birthday, radio.

Media Control

The Spectacular Achievements of Propaganda
by Noam Chomsky

1992; 21 pp.
$8 ppd (foreign $9) from: Open Magazine Pamphlet Series, P.O. Box 2726, Westfield, NJ 07091; 908-789-9608

There are two basic ideas central to Noam Chomsky's view of contemporary U.S. media. The first is propaganda, specifically the manipulation of public opinion by the creative use of history and images. Chomsky believes in the total victory of propaganda in U.S. media, and backs up his beliefs with examples from the run up to the Gulf War. Chomsky points to, for instance, the near total absence of the Iraqi opposition parties—who were opposed both to Hussein and the war—from the U.S. press as war talk heated up.

Chomsky's second idea centers on what he calls "spectator democracy," in which a seemingly democratic power structure is divided into two camps: a small, elite "specialized class" and a much larger group of everyday slobs, "the bewildered herd." It's the control of the herd that's at the heart of "spectator democracy." A small cadre of intellectually superior *uber*democrats use propaganda to mold the opinion—"manufacture consent"—among us knuckle-dragging street apes to haul us into the glittering future the specialized class knows is waiting for us, if only we had the balls and brains to follow them.

As with much of Chomsky's writing, **Media Control** is by turns infuriating, fascinating, and harrowing. No one who is interested in the uses of modern media and communication should miss this short, potent pamphlet.

In the Realms of the Unreal

"Insane" Writings

edited by John G. H. Oakes

1991; 253 pp.
$15.45 ppd (NY residents add sales tax) from: Four Walls Eight
Windows, P.O. Box 548, Village Station, NY, NY 10014; 800-835-
2246, ext. 123

Every culture has its own theories about what to do with the "mentally disturbed." In the West, we tend to lock them in hospitals,
which lets us give up on understanding the "insane." But the voice-
hearers, the babblers, and the automatic scribblers in the lock-down
wards have not given up on us. They've left behind reams of poetry,
stories and essays. **In the Realms of the Unreal** brings together
writings by "lunatics" from the U.S., Switzerland, Austria, Germany
and France. If you've ever wondered what it would be like to see
the world through new eyes and hear it through new ears, here's
your chance.

- *Adolf Wolfli: It should however, still be mentioned here that, in 1868,
  together with my very own parents and brothers and sisters as well as
  with their numerous friends, relations and acquaintances and directly
  accompanied by God, the Allmighty Fatther (sic), I climbed right to the
  very highest altitude of the 995 hours high Siiriuss-Rage on the planet
  of the same name on a gigantic Sorrantton (Heavenly Paradise-Bird)
  but during the descent, from approximately half the height: Which
  means from definitely no less than about: 485 hours,* I fell down the
  glittering, glistening rock face, which at this point juts out rather
  strongly, only to be snatched right out of mid-air down below and thus
  saved by a hard-working, deft giant cellar worker whom God the
  Allmighty Fatther had Personally alarmed and drawn his attention to
  me. O, how I wish that, under the very own miraculous guidance of
  God the Allmighty Fatther I could see everything once more, yes, really
  everything which I saw, lived through, suffered and experienced on the
  whole of the Globe, yes, even in quite a considerable part of the whole,
  immeasurable Universe, during those approx. 6 years from 1864, the
  year of my birth, until 1870: With the exception of those innumerable,
  mainly gigantic catastrophes. O time of youth, o happy time. (1913)*

  *1 hour = approx. 5000 m.

  Translated by Kiko Gaskell and Peter Jones

The Man Who Tasted Shapes

by Richard E. Cytowic, M.D.

$21.95; Tarcher/Putnam
1993; 249 pp.

The Mind of a Mnemonist

by A. R. Luria

$7.95; Harvard University Press
1968; 160 pp.

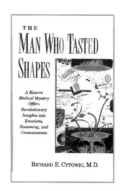

For close to 20 years, neurologist Richard E. Cytowic has been studying the perceptual anomaly known as *synesthesia*. Synesthetes (people with synesthesia) are individuals whose senses are mixed and combined in different ways. They can literally see sounds, taste shapes, and smell colors. By studying 40 synesthetes, Cytowic has come to some interesting conclusions about reality (there isn't really one objective one) and our perception of it (the world is much more subjective an experience than we've been taught). The implications of his ideas could change everything from art to science.

The Mind of a Mnemonist is A. R. Luria's case study of a single synesthete. Luria's patient manifested his switched-around senses in an unusual way—he became a *mnemonist*. A man who remembered everything. By combining the heightened sensory information afforded him by his synesthesia, Luria's patient was a walking encyclopedia of his own experience, but at a high price. Since he remembered everything, nothing mattered to him. Every event and scrap of data was equal. He never developed the ability to remember important facts, and discard the unimportant.

These two books point the microscope of perception back at our own minds and show us that what we "know" and what we "feel" are very individual sensations. In a world of fluid reality, then, we are free to create our own realities and not be the prisoners of perception—our own or anyone else's.

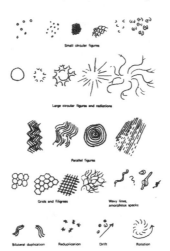

Generic shapes are common to synesthesia, hallucinations, migraine auras, and imagery, and can also be seen in primitive art. From M. J. Horowitz, used by permission. Image Foundation & Psychotherapy, p. 200; Hillsdale, NJ.

Lucid Dreaming

The Power of Being Awake and Aware in Your Dreams
by Stephen LaBerge, Ph.D.

1986; 304 pp.
$6.95 ppd ($10.95 foreign; CA residents add sales tax) from:
Lucidity Institute, 2555 Park Boulevard, # 2, Palo Alto, CA 94306;
800-465-8243; in CA 415-321-9969; fax 415-321-9967

Who needs to shell out money for drugs when your dreams are free?

Lucid Dreaming is the story of a system that allows you to "awaken" in your dreams, participate in them and control their outcomes. Author LaBerge isn't some New Age infomercial huckster; he's a scientist at the Stanford University Sleep Research Center, and an avid practitioner of lucid dreaming. Aside from learning how the system came into being, **Lucid Dreaming** gives you the basic techniques that allow you to dream lucidly on your own.

LaBerge is also the founder of the Lucidity Institute, which has courses, publications and devices such as the DreamLight and NovaDreamer, which aid in lucid dreaming. Contact them at the address above for a free catalog.

- *Non-lucid dreamers perceive themselves as being contained within the experiential worlds of their dreams....In contrast, lucid dreamers realize that they themselves contain, and thus transcend, the entire dream world and all of its contents, because they know that their imaginations have created the dream. So the transition to lucidity turns dreamers' worlds upside down. Rather than seeing themselves as a mere part of the whole, they see themselves as the container rather than the contents. Thus they freely pass through dream prison walls that only seemed impenetrable, and venture forth into the larger world of the mind.*

Technicians of Ecstasy

Shamanism and the Modern Artist
by Mark Levy
$14.95; Bramble Books
1993; 342 pp.

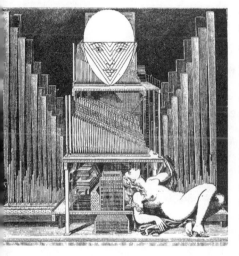

After 30 years of studying shamanic traditions in Asia, Europe and the Americas, author Mark Levy has come up with his own criteria for calling someone a shaman: 1) the shaman can call up alternate states of consciousness at will (i.e., a kind of conscious dreaming); 2) the shaman serves the "community and fulfill(s) vital needs"; 3) the shaman is the link between the secular and sacred worlds, rendering "divinely inspired" messages in ways that can be understood by everyone. These are the same characteristics of the artist in contemporary society.

Max Ernst collage, 1929.

In **Technicians of Ecstasy,** Levy examines the shamanistic techniques of such visionary modern artists as Giorgio de Chirico, Salvador Dali, Sha Sha Higby, Karen Finley, and Max Ernst, often in their own words.

- *Max Ernst: One rainy day in 1919, finding myself in a village on the Rhine, I was struck by the obsession which held under my gaze the pages of an illustrated catalogue showing objects designed for anthropologic, microscopic, psychologic, mineralogic, and paleontologic demonstration. There I found brought together elements of figuration so remote that the sheer absurdity of that collection provoked a sudden intensification of the visionary faculties in me and brought forth an illusive succession of contradictory images, double, triple and multiple images, piling up on each other with the persistence and rapidity which are peculiar to lover memories and visions of half-sleep...thus I obtained a faithful fixed image of my hallucination and transformed into revealing dramas my most secret desires—from what had only been some banal pages of advertising.*

Freaks

Myths and Images of the Secret Self
by Leslie Fiedler
$12.95. Anchor Books
1978; 367 pp.

Freaks

We Who Are Not As Others

by Daniel P. Mannix

1990; 120 pp.
$17.99 ppd (foreign $19.99; CA residents add sales tax) from:
RE/Search, 20 Romolo St., Ste. B, San Francisco, CA 94133

"Human curiosities," *mirabilia hominum* (human marvels), "monster," "prodigies" and "mutations" are all names for what we generically call "freaks." Whatever you think of the words used to describe these people who are so physically *other*, the fact is the cultural relationship between "freaks" and "normals" is long and complex. Since the Victorian era, ordinary people have been fascinated with "freaks" as a yardstick by which they could judge their own normality. Before that, Frederick I of Prussia had a habit of press-ganging anyone taller than seven feet into his service. He blithely kidnapped any so-called giants who didn't want to play along, and if they died on the way to Frederick's castle, he would just keep their bones for display. At the height of the Roman Empire, deformed babies were ritually killed as carrying the "evil eye." The Egyptian gods Bes and Ptah were depicted as dwarves. The Greeks displayed dwarves at fests, naked and decked in jewels. Even the medieval Europeans, who had made dwarves into court jesters, attributed magical powers and wisdom to them. In the 20th century, we pretty much relegated "freaks" to circuses and carny side-shows.

Leslie Fielder's **Freaks** looks at our complex cultural relationship with "freaks," as religious icons, as objects to pity and ridicule, as literary figures, as psychological archetypes, and as individual people.

Daniel P. Mannix's **Freaks** profiles many of the "freaks" he met and heard about while working as a sword-swallower and fire-eater in a traveling carnival. You'll find stories of General Tom Thumb, the two-foot tall dwarf who amused Queen Victoria, Percilla Bejano, the bearded "Monkey Woman," and Frank Lentini, who was proud of his third leg, and was equally ashamed of the thumb growing from it.

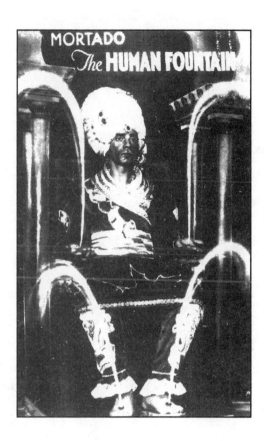

from **Freaks: We Who Are Not As Others.** Mortado, "The Human Fountain," at Coney Island, 1930. He had holes bored in his hands and feet, then inserted silver pipes and by means of pressure was able to squirt water through them.

- In our ancestors' awareness of Siamese Twins, the myth of the double merged with that of the multiple monster to create a myth of the Monstrous Self and an identically Monstrous Other joined together till death do them part. And this myth created a frisson no longer available to us, alas, even when confronting those who have chosen not to be separated. Recalling older show Freaks, however, who still felt themselves "chained for life," we can almost, almost re-create the original thrill. I myself think first of Daisy and Violet Hilton, who made a film with that grim title, and were perhaps for that reason chosen to represent their kind in Tod Browning's Freaks. THE STORY OF THE LOVE LIFE OF THE SIDESHOW, its publicity posters were headed, and the first question which followed, taking precedence over "Can a full grown woman love a midget?" and "What sex is the half man half woman?" was "Do Siamese twins make love?"

The Mole People

by Jennifer Toth

$19.95; Chicago Review Press
1993; 267 pp.

Where do you go when you're homeless, unable to find work and slip through enough cracks in the social system that you give up on the regular world just as surely as it's given up on you? If you're in New York, you might go underground—literally. Into the miles of deserted subterranean spaces—abandoned subway tunnels, water mains, sewage lines, and electrical conduits—that honeycomb the city. Some of you will live alone, by choice or because your mental problems make it hard for you to get along with other people. Some of you will form groups and construct small communities in the darkness. **The Mole People** is a look at cast-off individuals and groups who struggle every day to hold on to the small piece of land they've staked out for themselves, and the street violence, poverty, drug addiction, shortages in housing and support services that turned them into long-term urban spelunkers.

• *He (Gary Bass) enters the tunnels through emergency exits to the street, which by law cannot be sealed. One exit hatch that lifts a section of the Broadway sidewalk is part of the roof of his home, a duplex spanning two levels of the subway. The stairs to the lower floor are well swept, and the living quarters neat. His clothes drape neatly on hangers from a pipe. He shows me his working iron plugged into the tunnel's electrical system, standing atop a full-size ironing board. To read, he detaches the exit sign over a naked bulb to get its strong light. To sleep, he unscrews the bulb for complete darkness....The entrance off the tunnel is marked by crossed brooms and guarded by a trip wire that can bring down a five-gallon water bucket, which is sometimes full and sometimes empty but always warns of an intrusion....*

Japanese Jive

by Caroline McKeldin

$9.95. Tengu Books
1994; 48 pp.

Japanese Jive is a collection of photos of Japanese products, with bit of information and silly, occasionally sneering, commentary. Most of the products in **Japanese Jive** have English-language names, but the words are used in such mysterious combinations that their meaning is obliterated (much like the English on Japanese t-shirts). What do you suppose food products such as "Fish Ham" and "Black Black" really are?

Some of the products, however, reveal interesting sides of Japanese culture. For instance, blood type supposedly determines your personality; appropriately, in Japan you can get a condom that matches your blood type. You can also purchase

"Nippless," a tape to hide those protruding nipples. "Eye Talk" is perhaps the most disturbing product mentioned; it's an eyelid glue to give Japanese almond eyes a rounder, more Western look. **Japanese Jive** is not only interesting as a glimpse of foreign consumer culture, but it's a reminder that knowing the words of another language is a far cry from really understanding it.

Dear Mr. Ripley

edited by Mark Sloan, Roger Manley, Michelle Van Parys

$19.95; Bulfinch Press
1993; 205 pp.

If you've ever encountered someone doing something really stupid and wanted to tell them, "Get a life," don't bother. Here's a book that proves that no matter how bizarre, dangerous or stupid your hobby, someone (in this case, the famous Mr. Ripley of *Believe It or Not!* fame) will care, and document you doing it. You can feast your eyes on a guy who could kill, pluck, cut up, cook, and eat a chicken in less than two minutes, a guy who could lift 200 pounds with his nipples, guys and gals who stuck soldering irons and blow torches to their tongues, a woman who knit a hat from her own hair and...well, you get the idea. The toughest part about a book like this is figuring out who's crazier—the people in the book or the people reading it?

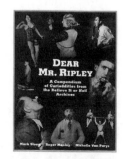

Believe It or Not! Man reads and reviews insane book!

The History of Hell

by Alice K. Turner

$29.95; Harcourt Brace & Co.
1993; 275 pp.

Detail of a 12th-century mosaic at Torcello. Note that a Byzantine Satan is as human as the Antichrist on his lap (upper right). Another Byzantine characteristic is the division of the damned into tidy compartments; Western Hells are more chaotic. The angels prod those whose headdresses betray their wealth and pride, while the Hellmouth is part of Satan's throne. Worms that never sleep are bottom left.

Just as the title says, this is a thoroughly researched (and fascinating) look at how religious leaders and street folk have thought about the underworld, or Hell. We start 4,000 years ago, with stories and poems about the Land of the Dead on Sumerian clay tablets and move through (primarily Christian) history and belief all the way up to the post-Freudian, neurosis-ridden twentieth century, stopping along the way to look in on the Gnostics, the Ancient Greeks, Dante, believers in a mechanical/Newtonian universe, Goethe and the Romantics.

- *What seems astonishing now is the literal bent theologians (in the Middle Ages) brought to matters that do not lend themselves to the literal. Intelligent, educated men, who, if they had been born centuries* later, might have explained the ineffable or metaphorical in terms of quarks and black holes in space, instead turned their attention to such considerations as whether food consumed during a lifetime would be part of the body at the resurrection. (Yes, was the answer, but then interesting questions of cannibalism arose.) "How many angels can dance on the head of a pin?" is the question theologians are supposed to have pondered, but they counted devils too and tried to calculate the size of Hell and where it is—under the earth or somewhere in the ether.

Saints Preserve Us!

by Sean Kelly & Rosemary Rogers
$10; Random House
1993; 343 pp.

As the authors of **Saints Preserve Us!** remind us, "...you don't have to be Catholic—or even Christian—to have Patron Saints." I was born on August 22, which, according to **Saints Preserve Us!**, means my Patron Saint is Symphorian, the protector of children and students, and who is invoked against syphilis. Hmm. I don't have any kids and was tossed out of school. On the other hand, I've never made friends with any spirochetes, so Saint Symphorian is hitting around 33% in my case. Of course, the Patron Saint of writers is John the Divine, that beast-watching boy-toy who gave us the Book of Revelations. Now there's a saint I can relate to!

Saints Preserve Us! gives you the dirt on saints for every day of the year, and also lists them alphabetically and by patronages (which includes Patron Saints for everything from truss makers to astronauts).

• **Fillian**—*January 19*

PATRON INVOKED AGAINST INSANITY

An eighth-century English hermit of Irish descent, who could (they say) study all night by the glowing of his left hand, Fillian had, during his lifetime, a calming effect on the mad. Long after his death (up until the nineteenth century) the mentally ill of Scotland were dipped in a pool (called Strathfillan) and left, tied up, overnight in the ruins of the Saint's chapel nearby. If they were found loose in the morning, they were considered cured.

Chick Tracts

$6.75 ppd (for a General Sample Pack) from: Chick Publications, P.O. Box 662, Chino, CA 91708-0662; 909-987-0771; fax 909-941-8128

Almost everyone who's walked down the streets of any major city has been handed a strange little rectangular comic known as a Chick Tract. Created by Jack Chick, these aren't just your run-of-the-mill pamphlets about accepting Jesus and loving God, they are twisted, fear-bloated, hate-spewing, the-end-is-nigh blasts of a true zealot. No one is spared, not scientists, feminists, gays, Muslims, the government, Catholics, the rich, rock musicians...The tracts make great party favors and, if you're a woman, try carrying a few around for self-defense. The next some idiot starts bugging you on the bus, hand him a tract and ask him if he's accepted Jesus as his personal savior. The guy will be gone, guaranteed.

Thee Psychick Bible

Thee Apocryphal Scriptures ov Genesis P-Orridge & Thee Third MIND ov Psychic TV
edited by J. A. Rapoza

1994; 175 pp.
$17.99 ppd (CA residents add sales tax) from: Alecto Ent.s, P.O. Box 460473, San Francisco, CA 94146; email: pyramid@well.com

Though it's called a Bible, this is more a collection of Genesis P-Orridge's essays, rants and ruminations, along with scriptures from previously published (though hard to find) Temple ov Psychick Youth and Psychic TV materials. Part Dadaist disquisition, and part philosophical manifesto ("**Thee Psychick Bible** is a call for self-actualization through rebellion...Rebellion against the forces and folks whose control is at the root of the schism between our conscious and unconscious minds."), this tome will probably be of greatest interest to anyone concerned in the more esoteric writings and ideas of Brion Gysin and William Burroughs, especially those laid out in their collaborative book, **The Third Mind.**

- *T.O.P.Y. Individuals believe that at thee instant ov orgasm, male or female, an hieroglyph symbolising a desire, a path, an awkwardness, can be in thee inner recesses ov thee mind, in what is commonly dubbed thee sub-conscious mind, but which T.O.P.Y. sees as thee REAL-CON-SCIOUS MIND. This act concentrates thee entire Individual upon contact with an achievement ov their desire. Thee patterns our brains inherit programme us. Observation and action, their cumulative effect through Invokation, are thee Process. We can internalise our programme, transmit a desire, receive a result.*

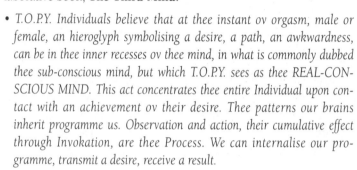

Smile Pretty and Say Jesus

The Last Great Days of PTL

by Hunter James

$22.95; University of Georgia Press
1993; 210 pp.

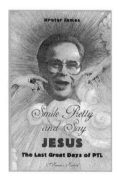

Reporter Hunter James covered Jim and Tammy Bakker and the PTL religion/money machine from the time the Jessica Hahn adultery story broke, until Jim's incarceration and his empire's demise. This is a classic reporter's tale, full of evangelistic hucksters, shifty lawyers, big money wheeling and dealing, end-of-the world true-believers, and crazed journalists circling like sharks who've smelled blood. The book is both entertaining and enlightening, as a look at big money religion, the complex loyalties at play in the legal world and the functioning of a press turned cynical and predatory, who have little interest in the ordinary people who had been swindled and who had seen their spiritual leader exposed as a thief and a creep.

Cinema Volta

by James Petrillo

$49.95; The Voyager Company
1994; requirements: color Macintosh; System 7; 13" monitor; 3 megs of RAM; CD-ROM drive

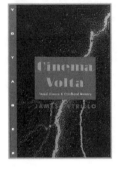

A cave painting of a bull. A cartoonish computer graphic of a woman's body. A bolt of lightning. A frog. A nude man. A ringing phone. The sound of crickets. The CD-ROM-based book, **Cinema Volta,** opens with a mini-movie composed of the nonlinear images and connections of dreams and memory. It's a stream-of-consciousness stroll through "weird science and childhood memory," all stitched together with the words and graphics of James Petrillo, an artist and teacher at CSU, Hayward.

What separates **Cinema Volta** from other disc-based books (and I've seen plenty) is the depth of its writing and its use of sound and graphics. The "book" is divided into chapters on such scientific luminaries as Volta, Morse, Edison, Bell, Tesla, and Lady Ada. These chapters are mingled with texts on Dante, Percy Shelley,

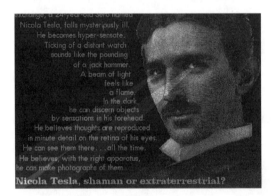

exchange, a 24-year-old Serb named Nicola Tesla, falls mysteriously ill. He becomes hyper-sensate. Ticking of a distant watch sounds like the pounding of a jack hammer. A beam of light feels like a flame. In the dark, he can discern objects by sensations in his forehead. He believes thoughts are reproduced in minute detail on the retina of his eyes. He can see them there. . .all the time. He believes, with the right apparatus, he can make photographs of them.

Nicola Tesla, shaman or extraterrestrial?

Frankenstein (both book and movie), and James Joyce's squeeze, Nora. Within each of these chapters we get a mixture of historical facts and odd, dreamlike connections. The chapter on Shelley incorporates both Lord Byron and Mary Shelley's writing of the Frankenstein story. The Frankenstein chapter brings together images of the Victor Frankenstein, his monster, computer nerds and Petrillo's father. The stylishly laid out text of the Frankenstein chapter, melts seamlessly into the chapter on Samuel Morse, then flows on to introduce Lady Ada (presented as a sexy, Warholian Bride of Frankenstein), which relates back to her father, Lord Byron....

Cinema Volta is set up so that you can read the chapters in any order you wish. One very nice option allows you to click a button and have your computer read the book to you. You'll begin with the author's ruminations on the ancient cave paintings at Lascaux, move through his life, his personal memories and memories of famous inventors, artists and monsters, and circle back to the author himself, wondering about the nature of the machine that's letting you read **Cinema Volta**, the first disc-based book for grown-ups that makes you believe that there's a future for more books of this type.

Eastgate Systems

information free from: Eastgate Systems, P.O. Box 1307, Cambridge, MA 02238; 617-924-9044; orders 800-562-1638; email: eastgate@world.std.com

Probably the biggest independent publishers and distributors of hypertext books for Macs and Windows 3.1 (and later) systems. Some of the highlights from their catalog include **Marble Springs** by Deena Larsen, a long work of hypertext poetry, **Victory Garden** by Stuart Moulthrop, the intuitively (though not necessarily logically) hypertextual **In Small & Large Pieces** by Kathryn Cramer, and **Uncle Buddy's Phantom Funhouse** by John McDaid, a hypermedia work which extends beyond the computer screen and onto two related audio cassettes included in the package.

Eastgate Systems also publishes the disc-based zine, *The Eastgate Quarterly Review of Hypertext*. Subscriptions are $49.95 a year; individual issues are $19.95 each.

Xen Distractionism

by Matthew Rogers and John Unger

requirements: Macintosh Plus or better; Hypercard 2.1 or later; information from: Fool's Errand Editions, 943 Carol St., Ypsilanti, MI 48198; email: raven@cyberspace.org

A poetic and philosophical hypertext manifesto that's part koan, part Beat road story and part **T.A.Z.**-like blueprint for a new and weirder world order. Sort of a digital **Tao te Ching** for online Slackers.

Atomic Books, 229 W Read St., Baltimore, MD 21201; 410-728-5490; BBS 410-669-4179; catalog $2

"Literary Finds for Mutated Minds." Atomic Books is a store and mailorder biz that carries all manner of extreme books, comix, zines, etc. You want an endorsement? Filmmaker John Waters shops there. Their catalog and weekly new release list is available free via anonymous ftp: ftp clark.net:/pub/atomicbk/

Computer Literacy Bookshops, 2590 N. First St., San Jose, CA 95131; 408-435-0744; fax 408-435-1823; email: info@clbooks.com; catalog free

They carry just about every computer and digital tech books in print; also selected cyberculture zines and fiction.

CyberMatrix, 5037 8th Road South, Arlington, VA 22204; 703-379-9234; email: ce930@po.cwru.edu

Cyberpunk books and zine source. They also carry computer hardware, videos and personal electronics. Catalog is only available online.

Delectus Books, 27 Old Gloucester St., London WC1N 3XX, U.K.; 081-963-0979; fax 081-963-0502; catalog $5 (U.K. £2; Asia, Australia and New Zealand $10)

Best source for rare, obscure, and hard-to-find British and European erotica. Modern books can go for as little as £3, while rare ones (some from 17th century) can go for over £300.

Hanuman Books, P.O. Box 1070, Old Chelsea Station, NY, NY 10113; email:bigpink@well.sf.ca.us; catalog free

Publishers of small, beautifully produced chapbooks with works by Patti Smith, William Burroughs, Jean Genet, Richard Hell, Jack Kerouac, etc. You can request a catalog by writing to the address above, or sending an email request. They also have t-shirts of some of their writers and original Hanuman designs.

I N C U N A B U L A, 415-241-1568; catalog free via email

"A Catalogue of Rare Books, Manuscripts & Curiosa, Conspiracy Theory, Frontier Science & Alternative Worlds." Incunabula isn't very forthcoming with info about themselves. They are a book, pamphlet, and broadsheet source for true-believers and those deeply interested. That means you have to be willing to go through some effort to get it. Currently their catalog exists in four parts on the gopher at well.com, in the section "Authors, Books, Periodicals, Zines (*Factsheet Five* lives here!)."

Left Bank Distribution, 4142 Brooklyn NE, Seattle, WA 98105; 206-632-5870; catalog $1

Left Bank carries an enormous range of alternative and small press titles, from politics to drugs, sexuality to science fiction.

Librairie le Scarabée D'Or, 61 rue Monsieur Le Prince, 75006 Paris, France; 46-34-63-61; fax 43-54-89-13; catalog free in Europe

Hard-to-find erotic prose and art books. Most of their books and zines are in French

Lindsay's Technical Books, P.O. Box 538, Bradley, IL 60915-0538; 815-935-5353; catalog $1

Reprints of 19th-century science books, DIY, self-sufficiency, weird physics, etc.

MediaKaos, 409 Laguna #4D, San Francisco, CA 94102; 415-241-1568; email: mediak@well.sf.ca.us

A small, but tasty selection of alternative titles concerning fringe science and politics. Also works by Genesis P-Orridge and Hakim Bey. Catalog is only available via email.

NEBULA,email: nebula@cam.org

Montreal-based science fiction bookstore now does mailorder. They stock a wide selection of North American, British and Australian SF books and zines. Their catalog is available via email. Send in your request with "catalog" in the subject field.

Paladin Press, P.O. Box 1307, Boulder, CO 80306; 800-872-4993; fax 303-442-8741; in Europe: CEP Europe, 70 Kingsdown Ave., Great Barr, Birmingham B42 1NF, England; 021-358-0628; catalog free

Combat tactics, military history, self-defense, law enforcement titles, also related videos.

Trails West, 1032 S. Boulder Rd, Louisville, CO 80027; 303-666-7107; catalog free

New, used, and out-of-print Americana and history; lots of obscure regional titles.

Voyager Expanded Books, 578 Broadway, NY, NY 10012; 800-446-2001; catalog free

Voyager books on floppy disk allow you to mark pages, enter margin notes, do extensive searches and mark passages. Their titles include fiction (Douglas Adams, Marge Piercy, William Gibson), non-fiction (John McPhee, Randy Shilts, Susan Faludi), as well as modern classics. Some books include extras such as the dinosaur illos and sounds on Voyager's Expanded Book version of **Jurassic Park**.

TO THE UN-SUSPECTING HUMANS?

PLAY GUITAR IN 7 DAYS
OR MONEY BACK

TOP GUITARIST ED SALE'S famous
secret system teaches you to p
tiful song the first d
song by ear or note
days! Contains 52 phot
ger placing charts, 110 p
western songs, (words and
$1.00 Chord Finder of all the c
in popular music; a $3.00 Guit
of Knowledge, TOTAL VALUE $7.0
—ALL FOR ONL
SEND NO MONEY! Just your nam
dress, pay postman $2.98 plus C
age. Or send $3.00 with order and
age. (Sorry, no C.O.D. outside
U.S.A.—please remit with order).
Unconditional Money-Back Gua
ED SALE
STUDIO195M AVON BY THE SEA,

COMIX

Introduction—Comix

Every few months, the advertising intelligentsia tries to get Americans to reinvent themselves. They do this by building a campaign around an idea or a word: ninja, the Sensitive Man, Super Mom, "smart" anything (card, tires, drugs, whatever). As I write this, the mega-marketing word of the week is "multimedia." The big money boys aren't really interested in defining the word, they're just hoping that if they shout it loud enough and long enough, you'll come across with beaucoup dollars so they can cruise for underage runaways in their BMWs while dreaming up next month's campaign.

The fact is, multimedia has been with us for a long time—really, ever since the first Neanderthal scrawled a picture on a cave wall to tell a story. One hundred thousand years later people are still drawing pictures to tell stories, only now we call them comic books. Yes, comix are the penny-pincher's route to multimedia extravaganzas. It's a great form. Think about it. Like a book, you can weave an intricate and diabolical plot to drive your readers crazy and keep them trembling in anticipation, or you can toss plot away, letting your characters' interactions move the story along, flowing with the unexpected turns and surprises of everyday life.

Like a movie, comix let you tell part of the story through pictures. Unlike a movie, however, you don't have budget problems. If you want to have a 600-foot jellyfish fall in love with the New Orleans Superdome, you can draw it, with as much detail as you want, and from as many angles as you can fit on a page. And you can have a cast of thousands. And they can be anything you want them to be: stocky cops, pale punks, talking dogs, three-fingered aliens, goofy robots or, god help us, ninja turtles.

You can start reading a comic anywhere you want. You can also stop reading it anywhere. You can dog-ear pages. You can look at your favorite parts over and over. And you don't need the $6,000 computer-based multimedia system the product floggers want you to buy.

The '80s saw the real comeback of comix as an interesting form. The DIY spirit of the contemporary zine world, along with the '60s idea that real life could fit into those pictures on a page gave the form the kick in the ass it needed. *Love & Rockets* by Los Brothers Hernandez was the title that lured back a lot of post-teenybopper readers who'd left comix behind. Now there are dozens of excellent titles available each month, and they cover a lot of ground. There's the satiric realism of *Hate* and *Cud*, the everyday realism of *Real Stuff* along with the poignant and ambitious *Signal to Noise*. *Raw* and *Snake Eyes* are as surreal and seemingly drug-addled as any '60s underground comic, and *Young Lust*, *Birdland* and *Real Girl* represent comix that bring together the unbridled lust of the '60s with a '90s polymorphously perverse viewpoint.

Welcome to the world of comix, the only multimedia system that comes off on your fingers.

The Comics Journal

$16/3 issues ($22 foreign) from: Fantagraphics Books, 7563 Lake City Way NE, Seattle, WA 98115; 800-657-1100; fax 206-524-2104

THE newszine of the comix world. Interviews, industry dirt, essays, great ads and fine art from elder statesmen such as Jack Kirby, and younger artists such as Diane Noomin.

Understanding Comics

The Invisible Art
by Scott McCloud

1993; 215 pp.
$23.85 ppd (MA residents add sales tax; Canada $28.95; overseas $33.95) from: Kitchen Sink Press, 320 Riverside Dr., Northampton, MA 01060; 800-365-7465; fax 413-586-7040

The history and aesthetics of comix are all explained—in a comic book! Learn about the connection between modern comix and 3,000 year old hieroglyphics; find out why some comic artists depict characters with almost photographic realism while others opt

for a more "iconic" approach to faces, how comix panels can be used to show the passage of time, emotional states or—simplest of all—place, how comix are shaped by the act of seeing them and the differences between U.S., European and Japanese comic languages. Smart, funny and literate, **Understanding Comics** is a must-have for both old and new fans of the art of comix.

A History of Underground Comics

by Mark James Estren

$19.95; Ronin Publishing
1993; 319 pp.

A look at the comix (mostly) of the 1960s, the ones that, as a group, changed the American form and attitude about comix forever. Rather than opting for a simple chronological approach to the subject, author Estren looks at comix according the themes and taboos they were playing with: sex, violence, drugs, "The World around Us," etc. One real plus for the book is that it doesn't try to explain things without showing you examples. **A History of Underground Comics** contains 1,000 illustrations, including all the big players: R. Crumb, Gilbert Shelton, S. Clay Wilson, Trina Robbins, Rick Griffin, Spain Rodriguez, Skip Williamson, and on and on. A reference book, a history book and a tribute to the restless imaginations and originality of a group of artists who were working to invent themselves.

- *In its most constructive form, this sort of (political) anger is channeled into a cartooning philosophy, as in the case of Justin Green: "There is a statement of Jung's that at puberty the initiate male must adopt the adult value system to displace the blissful childhood world; and when there is aberration or incomplete assimilation, neurosis resolved. Cartoons, particularly the animal variety, afford an ideal vehicle for mimicking the goals of society in a simplistic childhood way." But even in its most constructive form, the political consciousness of the underground cartoonists invariably comes from a sense of how wrong things are more than a sense of how to make them right—a fact which has led Harvey Kurtzman to remark, "The whole underground movement is so fucking anarchistic. Anarchy may be a lot of fun, but it carries within itself the seeds of its own destruction."*

A Small Killing

by Alan Moore & Oscar Zarate

$15.95 ppd (OR residents add sales tax; $26.95 foreign) from: Dark Horse Comics, 10956 SE Main, Milwaukie, OR 97222; 503-652-8815; 800-862-0052

A dense, fragmented look at the life, death and birth of an individual soul. Timothy Hole is an English-born ad wiz working in America. Then he gets his big break: he's to go to Russia and come up with a campaign for a new soft drink. Everything is great, except for two things. Tony's life is shit. He's walked away from the few women in his life that meant anything to him. His friendships are shallow business connections. He's not even sure if he should be in the advertising business. His other problem is even larger: it looks as if someone is trying to kill him. A child? A midget? Some weird ringer sent in by a rival ad firm to throw him off? Tim doesn't know, but he does know that the killer has followed him from the U.S. to Europe and is stalking him...

The text by Alan Moore, of *Watchmen* fame, is complex and assured, allowing much of the story to come through implication. Oscar Zarate's stylish rendering of Timothy's Hole's life and memories is a fine complement, a perfect yin to Moore's yang.

Birdland

by Gilbert Hernandez

$12.95 ppd (WA residents add sales tax) from: Eros Comics, P.O. Box 25070, Seattle, WA 98125; 800-657-1100; fax 206-524-2104

So there's this guy, an accountant. He loves his job and he's good at it. Other accountants judge their work against his and show him their spreadsheets in hopes of winning his approval. Now this same guy also likes to, say, play the horses. Some of his fans are shocked, some disappointed but he's having a hell of a great time figuring the odds and making lots of dough. Something about having cake and eating it springs to mind.

Gilbert Hernandez is like this guy. He and his brother Jaime's highly-acclaimed comic book *Love and Rockets* had been shepherding a loyal flock for years when *Birdland* first appeared. Originally released as a three-part series in 1990 and now in its second printing as a graphic novel, *Birdland* is Gilbert's racehorse. With it he embraces the carnal so enthusiastically, it can only be described as a labor of love.

The plot is a porn version of the old J. Geils song "Love Stinks." She loves him, he loves somebody else, etc. It's not just the story that's hot, but the storytelling that makes *Birdland* so successful. The characters are vividly strange twists on familiar icons: the inhumanly sexy stripper with a space alien fixation, the huge-membered brother in-law with a lisp fetish, and the hirsute, eternally erect, and hopelessly sappy protagonist. Witty and literate, every page bursts and drips with distended organs and bodily fluids.—Paul Kimball

Birdland is the first of a line of adult graphic titles from Eros Comics. There are now over a dozen books in all. Some other outstanding titles are *The Blonde, Talk Dirty* and *Lann*. The Eros Comics catalog is available for $2 from the same address as *Birdland*.—R.K.

Blab!

information from: Kitchen Sink Press, 320 Riverside Dr., Northampton, MA 01060; 800-365-7465; fax 413-586-7040

This pintsize paperback comic mag started out as a zine by and about underground comix and has evolved over the last few years into a memorable comic in its own right. Editor Monte Beauchamp has persuaded top alternative cartoonists such as Richard Sala, Doug Allen, Spain, and Dan Clowes to contribute some of their best work to each special-themed issue. He combines this with sprightly pop culture articles on topics like Bazooka Joe bubblegum comix, interviews with artists, and snappy graphic design. The result is personal publishing at its best. *Blab!* comes out every year or so and is well worth the wait.—Jay Kinney

Counter Parts

information from: Tundra Publishing, 320 Riverside Dr., Northhampton, MA 01060

Counter Parts is one of the weirdest comix around today. The story line is set in a future where personality is literally a commodity, purchased in capsule form. The protagonists are/is a set of body parts (two arms, two legs, a head, and a torso) that all have individual identities and varying personalities. They/it is pitted against the goverment(?) and the corporation that produces the personality drug, known as TPG. One of the funnier touches is the fact that even the "resistance" uses TPG, walking around spouting mechanical recitations of Che Guevera and Thomas Jefferson! The artwork is a superbly detailed Cali-fine line shaky scrawl. The comic that uses M.C. Escher's statement "my work has nothing to do with reality" as its credo will leave you wondering if in fact it does.—Joseph Matheny

CUD

$15.50/issues 1-5 ppd from: Fantagraphics Books, 7563 Lake City NE, Seattle, WA 98115; 800-657-1100; fax 206-524-2104

Terry LaBan cut his teeth drawing political cartoons for socialist newsmag *In These Times,* and then spent his journeyman years producing a dozen issues of his unsung comic *Unsupervised Existence*. With *Cud,* Terry has turned up the heat and is going for broke. If you ignore the delights this hilarious comic has to offer and Terry is forced to take up sign-painting instead, you'll only have yourself to blame. *Cud* chronicles the bizarre tale of performance artist Bob Cudd, who first turned up as one of the minor characters in *Unsupervised Existence*, and has

since become wildly successful despite his tormented insanity. LaBan wields a pointed pen as he skewers the art world, show biz, urban bohemia, sex, and politics. If the daily funnies leave you feeling hungry, chew on some *Cud.*—Jay Kinney

Cute L'il Bunny In Bumland

by Sham Dingus

1994; 100 pp.

$12 pp. from: Anathema Enterprises, 2002-A Guadalupe St., #227, Austin, TX 78705

'Twas the eve of Nixon's death and in the cold, haughty atmosphere of the world's most corporate Kinko's sat a group of Austin zinesters. After giggling over Tricky Dick's demise, we got down to perusing the products of our nine-hour copying frenzy. One book floated to the surface—a bloated, Crayola-covered masterpiece entitled *Cute L'il Bunny In Bumland.*

Designed as a coloring book-cum-collage piece, this 100-page volume follows the frantic, depraved adventures of a singularly well-hung bunny and his vile companion, Pruneberry, the Magical Booger Elf. If you find Beavis & Butthead a trifle too puerile or naughty for your taste, avoid Cute L'il Bunny like the Black Death. Author/artist Sham Dingus is one sick fuck, and uses der Bunny to offend, insult, or merely annoy everyone possible. Self-consciously foul, racist, misogynist, and rabidly anti-Christian, this comic/text nightmare pinions its targets with goofy glee, rather than getting stuck in some surly retro-punk rut or basking in the hip darkness of gloom imagery.

Everything about *Cute L'il Bunny In Bumland* is just plain wrong, and I mean that as a compliment. Cute L'il Bunny crucifies Santa Claus, rapes a number of particularly helpless individuals, and does all kinda nasty stuff with J.C., our Lord and Savior. Highly recommended reading material for all low-brows and irrepressible dorks like yrs. truly, it's also a bitchin' coffee table book for folks with a penchant for deconstructing the inexcusably adolescent art-shit of today's poor l'il alienated youngsters.

Should you purchase *Cute L'il Bunny In Bumland* and find it tedious, unsettling or genuinely offensive, just think of what Sham Dingus would reply to your complaints: "Fuck Your Jesus!"—Tiffany Lee Brown

Dangle

Information from: Drawn and Quarterly, 5550 Jeanne Mance St. #16, Montreal, Quebec, CANADA H2V 4K6

Lloyd Dangle draws the weekly comic strip, *Troubletown*, which you may find hidden back in the classified ad pages of your local "alternative" paper. If you've seen it, you'll know that *Dangle* captures the repressed hostility of urban America perfectly. His loose pen line is jumpy and jittery and express-es the sardonic humor required to make it through the ravages of modern life. Dangle's self-titled comicbook presents his longer work, which is even better than the short *Troubletown* strips. This guy is hopelessly sardonic—in other words he tells the truth.—Jay Kinney

Eightball

$12.50/4 issues ppd from: Fantagraphics Books, 7563 Lake City NE, Seattle, WA 98115; 800-657-1100; fax 206-524-2104

Dan Clowes has my vote as the killer cartoonist of the '90s. Every few months a new issue of *Eightball* arrives full of ornery mockery of people who are all too real. Of special note is Clowes' pathetic superhero cartoonist "Young Dan Pussey" who lays bare the souls of comix fanboys everywhere. Also watch for Clowes' paperback collections: *Lout Rampage, Velvet Glove,* and *The Lloyd Llewellyn Collection.*—Jay Kinney

Hate

$18/6 issues ppd from: Fantagraphics Books, 7563 Lake City NE, Seattle, WA 98115; 800-657-1100; fax 206-524-2104

Peter Bagge is probably the most prolific cartoonist in the alternative comix scene. And, luckily, everything he produces is simultaneously funny and very human. Bagge was already chronicling the Seattle slacker scene back when no one but locals had ever heard of

Nirvana or Pearl Jam. His characters, Buddy Bradley, Girly Girl, Stinky, George Cecil Hamilton, Jr., Valerie, Lisa, form a soap operatic universe of crappy jobs, roommate warfare, doomed relationships, substance abuse, and rock illusions. Bagge's style might be called realistic slapstick. Warning: *Hate* is addictive.—Jay Kinney

Horny Biker Slut

$4/ea. ppd (CA residents add sales tax) from: Last Gasp, P.O. Box 410067, San Francisco, CA 94141-0067; 800-848-4277

Do I really have to explain this one? Read the title again. *Horny. Biker. Slut.* That's what this series is all about, only there's more than one slut in the comic. And these sluts know what they want. They want each other. They want the guys they hang out with. Sometimes they want disgusting, fat, sweaty pigs because...well, just because. *Horny Biker Slut* is filth, utter filth, wildly un-PC and hotter than the tailpipe of a Harley after the Sturgis run. Don't let your mom or the cops catch you with this one.

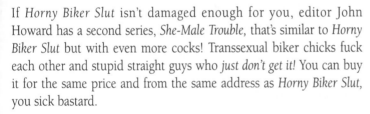

If *Horny Biker Slut* isn't damaged enough for you, editor John Howard has a second series, *She-Male Trouble,* that's similar to *Horny Biker Slut* but with even more cocks! Transsexual biker chicks fuck each other and stupid straight guys who *just don't get it!* You can buy it for the same price and from the same address as *Horny Biker Slut,* you sick bastard.

Hothead Paisan

Homicidal Lesbian Terrorist
$14/4 issues ppd from: Giant Ass Publishing, P.O. Box 214, New Haven, CT 06502

Even if you gave Wonder Woman a haircut, an *On Our Backs* sub-scription and a bad attitude, she still wouldn't be as cool as Hothead Paisan. Hothead is a combat boot-sporting, community supporting, establishment threatening, girl loving, spritz-head smashing everygirl superrr herrro. She's your Feminism 101 class on steroids. She's the only known antidote for the way you feel when some bike messen-ger passes you on the street with a "hey, baybee" and a smirk. She'd be Jesse Helms' worst nightmare if he had a brain to dream with. A feel-good bomb for the '90s in 2-D, *Hothead Paisan* is required read-ing for the revolution.—Daphne Gottlieb

Justine, Vols. 1 & 2

by Guido Crepax

$15.95 ea. ppd (NY residents add sales tax) from: NBM, 185 Madison Ave., #1504, NY, NY 10016; 800-488-8040

Even though they've metamorphosed, comic books still bear the vestiges of coming from a moral universe; to some degree, the form still presumes a world where good triumphs over evil, where heroes use superpowers to overcome adversity.

This tradition is supremely foiled with Guido Crepax's graphic novel adaptation of the Marquis de Sade's *Justine*. Pity poor Justine, as she travels down the road from riches to rags, clinging to shreds of her virtue and dignity, rewarded only with debasement and cruelty. Rendered exquisitely in black and white, Crepax's hand depicts the excesses of pre-revolutionary France, the sublime and the grotesque. The story unfolds almost cinematically, and the books powerfully embellish the original text. However, caveat to minors and those with weak stomachs for rape, sodomy and other explicit, non-consensual acts of cruelty.

Also available by Guido Crepax: *The Story of O, Dr. Jekyll and Mr. Hyde, Emanuelle,* vols. 1-3.—Daphne Gottlieb

Killer Komix

£8.49 ppd (UK £5.99; Europe £7.49; overseas £8.49) from: Headpress, P.O. Box 160, Stockport, Cheshire SK1 4ET, England

A British comic made up entirely of biographies of murderers, the famous and near famous: Charles Manson, Ed Gein, Jeffrey Dahmer, the Zodiac Killer, David Berkowitz, Richard Ramirez, etc. Twelve chapters, thirteen killers (the Lonely Hearts Killers were a couple). While some

of the bios don't incorporate the most recent findings and theories (for instance, it seems more likely from studying Berkowitz that he was faking his madness), these are a fine set of introductions to the crimes themselves. The drawing and prose styles of *Killer Komix* range from straight documentary realism to an almost manic primitivism. A fine piece of work for, as the song says, the devil inside.

Kim Deitch

information from: Fantagraphics Books, 7563 Lake City NE, Seattle, WA 98115; 800-657-1100; fax 206-524-2104

Kim Deitch has produced so many comix of varying titles that it makes more sense to list him by name rather than arbitrarily choosing just one of his books. Deitch is one of the few cartooning veterans of the old '60s underground press who is still at it and getting ever better. He has several favorite worlds that his characters inhabit including old-time Hollywood, the early days of cartoon animation, and a wacked out sci-fi universe of robots, monsters, and time travel. Think of Raymond Chandler writing and drawing Felix the Cat sequences for the Twilight Zone and you begin to get the picture. Kim's comix and paperback collections include *All Waldo Comics!*, *Beyond the Pale!*, *Hollywoodland!*, *No Business Like Show Business!*, and *Boulevard of Broken Dreams* .—Jay Kinney

Naughty Bits

$10/3 issues ppd from: Fantagraphics Books, 7563 Lake City NE, Seattle, WA 98115; 800-657-1100; fax 206-524-2104

Roberta Gregory first surfaced in the '70s with some classic lesbian/feminist comic fare such as *Dynamite Damsels* and then dropped from sight for a long stretch. In recent years she has come back stronger than ever (and way less politically correct) with her quarterly comic, *Naughty Bits*. Gregory's biggest character is Bitchy Bitch, the PMS-ridden date from hell who reveals the dark underside of modern womanhood that most women are loath to admit to. At turns excruciatingly funny and pointedly scathing, *Naughty Bits* is always honest.—Jay Kinney

The Magician's Wife

by Jerome Charyn & Francois Boucq

$17.95 ppd (NY residents add sales tax) from: NBM, 185 Madison Ave., #1504, NY, NY 10016; 800-488-8040

The Magician's Wife is part Svengali story, part coming of age tale and part Felliniesque fantasy. It's the story of Rita, a young girl, and Edmund, the magician son of a rich family, who says he loves her. Edmund is, by turns, childishly cruel and colorfully seductive. At one moment, Edmund can use his magic to torment Rita—like a spoiled older brother—and then conjure up talking animals or an elaborate 18th-century ballroom with masked guests. Rita has her own tricks, though, and when pushed too far, her fury transforms her into a wolf. Later, after Rita has left Edmund, she is implicated in a series of savage murders in a park. Has her hatred of Edmund made her lose control of the wolf inside her? Nothing is certain in *The Magician's Wife*. The world, through Rita's eyes, is cruel and fantastic, eerie and sensual. Compounded of themes of love, violence, mystery, luck, and the wisdom of ghosts, *The Magician's Wife* is for anyone who understands that it's through stories of the fantastic that we get many of our most realistic glimpses of life.

Peep Show

information from: Drawn and Quarterly, 5550 Jeanne Mance St. #16, Montreal, Quebec, CANADA H2V 4K6

The last few years have seen a spate of confessional first-person comix drawn in black and white by young obscure cartoonists. Joe Matt has pulled ahead of the pack by ruthlessly chronicling his rather ordinary life in mind-boggling detail. See Joe jerk off, break up with his girlfriend, act the tightwad, watch videos. Matt's comic *Peep Show* provides the uncanny experience of forced voyeurism on the life of someone who revels in revealing his own jerkiness. Start with Matt's *Peep Show* paperback collection of his early work and then plow into his quarterly comic for updates on his neuroses. Fascinating!—Jay Kinney

Raw, Vol. 3

High Culture for Lowbrows

ed. by Art Spiegelman & Francoise Mouly

$17.95 ppd (WA residents add sales tax) from: Fantagraphics Books, 7563 Lake City Way NE, Seattle, WA 98115; 800-657-1100; 206-524-1967; fax 206-524-2104

Art Spiegelman, creator of *Maus*, a personal history and Holocaust narrative featuring animals in all the prominent roles, has another claim to fame: *Raw*. This irregular series of anthology comix (co-edited with Francoise Mouly) brings together some of the most interesting, influential, experimental, straight-forward, funny, sad, and just plain cool comix writers and artists alive (and some dead ones, too; *Raw* has also reprinted some of George Herriman's *Krazy Kat* strips). No longer a comic magazine, but a trade paperback from Penguin Books, *Raw* has recently featured artists such as Lynda Barry, Drew Friedman, Kaz, Alan Moore, Kim Deitch, Mark Beyer, and, of course, Spiegelman himself. If you don't know much about modern comix, *Raw* is a fine place to start your education. It's also the title you can throw at any moron who still thinks comix are for kids.

Art Spiegelman continues *Maus*, his family Holocaust story in the latest issue of *Raw*.

Real Girl

Edited by Angela Bocage

$21/issues #1-6 ppd from: Fantagraphics Books, 7563 Lake City NE, Seattle, WA 98115; 800-657-1100; fax 206-524-2104

Donchya know that lesbians just hug and kiss a lot? Yeah, but *Real Girl* comix cover the queerness that subverts this stereotype and kicks the ass of the politically correct powers that be. This collection is so "out-there" that it includes a comic by Roberta Gregory that tells the story of a dyke and a fag falling in love. It shows all of the shit that they get from their queer friends for "selling-out" and going straight, the fear of playing with a wholly different set of genitals and the power dynamics of hetero sex.

A tender moment from "One Fine Night San Francisco Evening," by Fish in the new issue of *Real Girl*.

The drawings aren't that stimulating, but some of the stories are funny as hell. Check out "One Fine San Francisco Evening" by Fish which is a night in the life of a couple of butch bottoms who make the mistake of showing up on time for their appointment with their femme mistress. Most of the story lines are irreverent looks at queer lifestyle: cute, cuddly, assimilated lesbians won't be found in this collection. The comix are by various women and are touted on the cover as "The sex comic for all genders and orientations, by cartoonists who are good in bed." I can't vouch for the sexual prowess of any of the contributors (although I've heard rumors that verify this assertion), but I certainly agree that these comix don't so much have gender biases as they are pervert friendly.—Daryl-Lynn Johnson

The first four issues of *Real Girl* have been collected in one book. It's $13 postpaid, from the address above.—R.K.

Real Stuff & Real Smut

information from: Fantagraphics Books, 7563 Lake City NE, Seattle, WA 98115; 800-657-1100; fax 06-524-2104

These two comix are frontrunners in the autobiographical comix competition of the last several years. Dennis Eichhorn writes the stories (mostly) and some of the best subterranean cartoonists draw them. This is similar in premise to Harvey Pekar's *American Splendor Comics* (which has been around for years and has received ample coverage elsewhere).The big difference between the two is that Eichhorn has led a truly baroque and wide ranging life while Pekar's tales celebrate his own humdrum existence. Then again, maybe Eichhorn is just making it all up, but if so, he's still a great comix writer. Catch his work before he runs out of anecdotes!—Jay Kinney

She Comics

An Anthology of Big Bitch

by Spain Rodriguez and Algernon Backwash

$18.95 ppd (CA residents add sales tax) from: Last Gasp, P.O. Box 410067, San Francisco, CA 94141-0067; 800-848-4277

French vanilla ice cream and a little head are what every girl deserves after a hard day at work, and Big Bitch works harder than most girls; she's a hired gun. And she's not very discriminating; she just doesn't like rude men, limp dicks, or anti-porn feminists. Her motto is "Don't fuck with Big Bitch," but her favorite come-on is hiking up her skirt and fingering herself.

She Comics, drawn by comix veterans Spain Rodriguez and Algernon Backwash, is a collection of short strips that revolve around the life of Big Bitch, a super-spy. She does everything—from saving third-world countries to playing high-priced dominatrix to CEOs. This blonde is no young bimbo, but she has a high firm ass and tits like the French vanilla cones she is so fond of. Her manservant, Asquith, aides her in her capers and provides his tongue for her clitoral pleasure when the job is done. The strips are so short that Big Bitch seems to be wrapping up a case and sitting back with Asquith's head in between her legs every other page. While I'm all for women getting as much head as possible, I'd feel a little more satisfied if she worked a little harder for the money.—Daryl-Lynn Johnson

Signal to Noise

by Neil Gaiman & Dave McKean

information from: Dark Horse Comics, 10956 SE Main, Milwaukie, OR 97222; 503-652-8815; 800-862-0052

Signal to Noise is about as grown-up as a comic can get. It's so far from the world of funny animals and superheroes, you can find yourself groping for other things to call it. The color storyboards for a film that doesn't, but ought to, exist? A multimedia cut-up? There's always the dreaded nom-de-guerre, "graphic novel." All these names apply.

Signal to Noise is about the end of the world, about the idea of "the end of the world." There are many versions of the apocalypse available to us in the late 20th century. As the millennium approaches,

there's the real end to a thousand-year cycle of human time. There is also the possible end of the world that is prophesied every thousand years by religious zealots. And there is cancer, a very personal, but no less real end to the world. *Signal to Noise* looks at all these possible scenarios through the thoughts of a dying film director, an artist who will never finish his last project. The meaning of his life, his death and the end of the world consume him. While this is a story about despair, it's not despairing. Our lives are full of little apocalypses, events and ideas that destroy our old selves, and give birth to new ones. Like any good book, reading *Signal to Noise* will leave you a little changed, meaning that like any good book, it will kill you. Another little apocalypse.

Slutburger

information from: Drawn and Quarterly, 5550 Jeanne Mance St. #16, Montreal, Quebec, Canada H2V 4K6

Mary Fleener's mostly first-person tales, drawn with a firm well-controlled line, are always enjoyable (and sometimes wicked) looks at life in Southern California. Fleener's art sometimes leaps into cubism or visual poetry, and at other times strictly sticks to telling a funny story. The timeframe ranges from the '60s to the '90s, the worldview is left coast bohemian, and the tone is frank. As is typical in the alternative comix scene, Mary puts far more sweat into her art than she'll ever earn back in royalties.—Jay Kinney

Snake Eyes

$12.95 ppd (WA residents add sales tax) from: Fantagraphics Books, 7563 Lake City NE, Seattle, WA 98115; 800-657-1100; fax 206-524-2104

Every couple of years a new issue of *Snake Eyes* appears and it is always a cause for celebration. Full of cartoonists like Kaz, Mark Newgarden, and Mark Beyer, who were (for my money) the best artists to appear in *Raw*, as well as other smart alecks like Glenn Head, Julie Doucet, and Roy Tompkins who've made their marks elsewhere, this paperbound comic anthology is reliably raucous and raunchy. Most of these artists teeter on the thin line between surrealism and insanity, but they know how to crank out well-crafted tales that suck you into their twisted little fever-dreams.—Jay Kinney

Squeak the Mouse, Vols. 1 & 2

$13.95 ea. ppd (NY residents add sales tax) from: NBM, 185 Madison Ave., #1504, NY, NY 10016; 800-488-8040

Sometimes after you see a movie you hear that there's a "European cut"—a longer, more adult version with the sex and violence left intact. *Squeak the Mouse* is sort of the "European cut" of *Tom and Jerry*, a sophisticated combo-pack of humor, porn, and ultraviolence. Throughout the two books, Squeak and his unnamed cat nemesis go through all the typical cat and mouse cartoon scenarios—blowing each other up, smacking each other with blunt objects—only in this Euro-version, the cute cartoon characters bleed, get compound fractures, and exact awful revenge on each other. And, being the cartoon adults they are, Squeak and the cat have sex as often as possible. Like the violence, the sex is funny (cat and mouse cluster fucks, frat boy tongue wrestling, etc.) and rendered in exquisite detail.

Too Much Coffee Man

information from: Adhesive Comics, P.O. Box 5372, Austin TX 78763-5372

Too Much Coffee Man is a sometimes cynical, sometimes quirky, always amusing comic from the fertile mind of Shannon Wheeler. The artwork exudes that uncomfortable feeling of being gacked to the gills on java and the writing has a quality of, well, too much coffee. *TMCM* explores everything from the overuse of cliches in the traditional hero comic to the complexity of relationships. What sets it apart from the rest of the pulp-mill dribble is the aura of "3 a.m. and I can't sleep so I might as well draw" it transmits, both in style and content. So get a big cup of the heart of darkness, curl up in your favorite chair and have a tweak fest with *Too Much Coffee Man.*—Joseph Matheny

Young Lust #8

$5.95/ea. ppd (CA residents add sales tax) from: Last Gasp, P.O. Box 410067, San Francisco, CA 94141-0067; 800-862-0052

From Last Gasp comes an anthology from the old school of underground comix. *Young Lust #8* features some big names and some very funny stories. Terry LaBan's "Modern Primitive" is an over-the-top portrayal of the tattoos-and-piercing set, while Bill Griffith's "Zippy the Pinhead" appears in an explicit situation comedy that's as pornographic as they come. Other superior work is presented by editor Jay Kinney, Harry S. Robbins, Angela Bocage, Charles Burns and Diane Noomin. Most of the stories travel well-charted satirical territory, but the creative talents behind these pieces make them fresh.—Paul Kimball

Bill Griffith's "Zippy the Pinhead" gets a pornographic workout in the newest issue of *Young Lust.*

EZINES

Introduction—Ezines

Zines are mostly small-scale, independent publications produced by non-professionals—people who have some obsession, idea, or image they want to get across to other people. Some zines concentrate on graphics, and others on words. Some are uplifting, some informational, and some a deranged smut fest. Zines are as wild and varied as the people who produce them. We looked at 100 or so print zines in the first **Covert Culture Sourcebook**. In **CCS 2.0**, we're concentrating on the print zines' etheric little brothers and sisters: ezines.

Ezines is short for "electronic zines," publications that come to you through the Internet, over a modem. Unlike print zines, ezines have one big advantage: production and distribution is practically free. You don't have copying, envelope stuffing, or postage costs, you're just pushing around electrons from your online system to someone else's system. Like traditional zines, ezines cover a wide variety of subjects, from poetry to terrorism, from Tibetan news to UFO rants, from the Internet to postmodern social theories.

Unlike print zines, ezines are only text. A few ezines have set up homepages on the World Wide Web. If you have the proper software and the proper type of online account (for instance, a SLIP account), you can access text, sound and graphics from your computer (for more info on the WWW, check out the chapter titled "The Net"). For most of the ezines listed here, however, all you need is basic Internet access and email. (A few of the ezines reviewed here also have print versions; those that do usually mention it at the beginning or the end of each issue.) .

Ezines

Ezines, or electronic-zines, are the net-based counterpart of traditional print-zines. Like printed zines, you can subscribe to most zines and receive them through email. Some ezines, however, don't email individual copies, and so you must download them from FTP sites. If you're not sure how to use FTP, consult one of the books reviewed on pages 122-123, or ask a customer service rep on your home system. Another place to find a particular ezine is in a related Usenet newsgroup. For many of the non-subscription ezines, this is the easiest place to find and download them.

A-albionic Research

subscription: postmaster@mail.msen.com

The A-albionic Research ezine is "a ruling class/conspiracy research resource for the entire political-ideological spectrum."

Alife Digest

subscription: journals-orders@mit.edu

The journal for the study of Artificial Life, a branch of Artificial Intelligence, that grew out of studies at the Santa Fe Institute of Complexity Research.

Amazons International

subscription: amazons-request@math.uio.no

"*Amazons International* is an electronic magazine for and about Amazons (physically and psychologically strong, assertive women who are not afraid to break free from traditional ideas about gender roles and femininity/"feminine interests and behavior"), and their friends and lovers. *Amazons International* is dedicated to the image of the female hero in fiction and in fact, as it is expressed in art and literature, in the physiques and feats of female athletes, and in sexual values and practices."

Ansible

subscription: ansible-request@dcs.gla.ac.uk

David Langford's witty ezine covering the British science fiction scene (with a little of the U.S. thrown in).

- *GENERAL MANUEL NORIEGA, interviewed by film-maker Oliver Stone, proves to be a fan. _OS:_ `What books do you read?' _MN:_ `I like science fiction very much.' _OS:_ `Any favourites?' _MN:_ `No,* *whatever, whatever.' _John Foyster_ adds: `Ya gotta admire Stone's dead sophisticated interviewing techniques, but what is Noriega trying to hide? A passion for Lois McMaster Bujold? David Drake? Etc? Is this worth a competition?'*

Arm The Spirit

subscription: aforum@moose.uvm.edu (in Subject field enter: ATS: e-mail request)

"*Arm The Spirit* is a anti-imperialist/autonomist collective that disseminates information about liberation struggles in advanced capitalist countries and in the so-called 'Third World.' Our focus is on armed struggle and other forms of militant resistance but we do not limit ourselves to this. In *Arm The Spirit* you can find news on political prisoners in North America and Europe, information on the struggles of Indigenous peoples in the Americas, communiqués from guerrilla groups, debate and discussion on armed struggle and much more. We also attempt to cover anti-colonial national liberation struggles in Kurdistan, Puerto Rico, Euskadi and elsewhere."

ART COM

subscription: artcom-request@well.sf.ca.us

"Welcome to ART COM, an online magazine forum dedicated to the interface of contemporary art and new communication technologies." Each issue has a guest editor.

"Other ART COM projects include:

"ART COM MAGAZINE, an electronic forum dedicated to contemporary art and new communication technologies.

"ART COM ELECTRONIC NETWORK (ACEN), an electronic network dedicated to contemporary art, featuring publications, online art galleries, art information database, and bulletin boards.

"ART COM SOFTWARE, international distributors of interactive video and computer art.

"ART COM TELEVISION, international distributors of innovative video to broadcast television and cultural presenters.

"CONTEMPORARY ARTS PRESS, publishers and distributors of books on contemporary art, specializing in postmodernism, video, computer and performance art."

For more information, email: artcomtv@well.sf.ca.us.

Bits and Bytes Online Edition

subscription: listserv@acad1.dana.edu (leave Subject field blank; on line by itself enter: subscribe bits-n-bytes)

"Bits and Bytes Online Edition will contain news of interest to anyone interested in the state of the computer industry, and more importantly, in the *future* of said industry, and by extension, the future directions of our increasingly high tech society.

"The format will be concise and informal. Many of the postings are taken directly from the online world and print media. I cannot predict what topics will be covered in any given issue: B&B is an experiment in progress.

"Here are *some* of the topics I'll be covering:

+ New products and services, with contact information.

+ Internet access and points of interest in the online world.

+ New and pending legislation at the national and local level.

+ Advances in science and technology.

+ Emerging paradigms in the way America (and the world) does business.

+ Civil liberties on the electronic frontier.

+ New technologies that will shape our leisure time. For example, 500 channel cable systems, interactive multimedia, and the rapid growth of the online world of the Internet and BBS systems.

+ Access to technical info (for all us programmer types).

+ Strange goings on in the digital universe.

+ Book, magazine and software reviews and listings."

Bleeding Edge

subscription: leavitt@armory.com

"Taking you where no one has gone before...to the obscure depths of truly alternative computing, where desperate users ponder the future, and stretch the capabilities of their machines to the utmost." Bleeding Edge editor, Thomas Leavitt, means that his zine concentrates on older workstations and computers other than Macs, PCs, and PC clones.

Blink

subscription: listserv@listserv.acns.nwu.edu (leave Subject field blank; on line by itself enter: subscribe blink)

"Blink would like to be a forum for the issues surrounding the

intersection of consciousness and technology. This is our best defense against postmodern angst: To critically look at and anticipate the cultural and social changes spurred by the rapid development of technology."

Chaos Control

FTP: world.std.com:/obi/Zines/Chaos.Control

"Focusing on electronic music. *Chaos Control* features interviews with both major and underground acts."

Choice-Net Report

subscription: dtv@well.sf.ca.us

"*Choice-Net Report* is a weekly update on reproductive rights issues distributed through email."

• RU486 TESTED FOR USE AS "MORNING AFTER" PILL

The University of California at San Francisco is one of 14 sites (and the only one in the U.S.) chosen for simultaneous clinical trials designed to test the effectiveness of RU486 as an emergency contraceptive....The goal of the study will be to determine the best dosage of the drug for preventing pregnancies. Women will be tested at three dosages up to five days after having unprotected sex. Possible side effects to RU486 include bleeding, nausea, dizziness, breast tenderness, and abdominal pain. RU486 is a steroid known also known as mifepristone and is most widely known for its ability to induce abortion by blocking the action of the hormone progesterone which is essential for beginning and maintaining a pregnancy. Women interested in participating in the trial may call 415-502-0299.

Computer Underground Digest

FTP: etext.archive.umich.edu:/pub/cud

"An open forum dedicated to sharing information among computerists and to the presentation and debate of diverse views." In Europe, FTP: ftp.warwick.ac.uk:pub/cud)

The CPSR Alert

subscription: listserv@gwuvm.gwu.edu (leave Subject field blank; on line by itself enter: subscribe cpsr first-name last-name)

"*The CPSR Alert*, the electronic newsletter put out by the CPSR Washington Office. The focus of the publication is electronic privacy, information access, FOIA and the NII."

Cropduster

FTP: etext.archive.umich.edu:/pub/Zines/Cropduster

"*Cropduster* revolves, as perhaps everything does, around the substance that one calls pop-culture. With various jargon thrown around including: post-modernism, nihilism, etc. in an attempt for one generation to understand the next, people forget what the essence of pop-culture really is—a collection of somewhat useless artifacts which are given exceptional value by groups of people. What we hope to show is not the trends but rather the idols of pop-culture. We hope to convey the simplicity of everyday life through the icons which lead generation upon generation onwards."

CTHEORY

subscription: listserv@vm1.mcgill.ca (leave Subject field blank; on line by itself enter: subscribe ctheory first-name last-name)

"*CTHEORY* is an international, electronic review of books on theory, technology and culture. Sponsored by the Canadian Journal of Political and Social Theory, reviews are posted monthly of key books in contemporary discourse as well as theorizations of major "event-scenes" in the mediascape. *CTHEORY* will also include the possibility of interactive discussions among its subscribers."

Discipline

subscription: toby@cs.man.ac.uk

"The weekly moderated email newsletter for discussing Robert Fripp's (and King Crimson's) music." This is for fans only. No flaming is allowed.

EFFector Online

subscription: eff-news-request@eff.org

The computer world/internet/information zine and mouthpiece for the Electronic Frontier Foundation, a lobbying and information group committed to keeping the Net as open and free as possible.

FineArt Forum

subscription: fast@garnet.berkeley.edu (leave Subject field blank; on line by itself enter: subscribe FineArt first-name last-name)

"*FineArt Forum* is an eight-year old internet-based newsletter serving art and technology."

Flash Information

subscription: flash@citi.doc.ca

"ISIR, the Integrated Service of Information Resources, of the Centre for Information Technology Innovation (Industry Canada) disseminates a selective bibliography and information briefs aimed at R&D managers, researchers, and professionals within the field of information technologies (computers and computing; software engineering; natural language processing; multimedia systems; information storage; interchange and retrieval; work organization; etc.)."

FUNHOUSE!

FTP: etext.archive.umich.edu:/pub/Zines/Funhouse

"Dedicated to whatever happens to be on my mind at the time I'm writing. The focus will tend to be on those aspects of our fun-filled world which aren't given the attention of the bland traditional media, or which have been woefully misinterpreted or misdiagnosed by the same. *FUNHOUSE!* is basically a happy place, and thus the only real criteria I will try to meet is to refrain from rants, personal attacks, and flames—and thus *FUNHOUSE!* is an apolitical place. Offbeat films, music, literature, and experiences are largely covered, with the one stipulation that articles are attempted to be detailed and well documented, although this is no guarantee of completeness or correctness, so that the interested reader may further pursue something which may spark her interest."

The Global Network Navigator

subscription: info@gnn.com

"*The Global Network Navigator,* a free Internet-based information center that will initially be available as a quarterly. GNN will consist of a regular news service, an online magazine, *The Whole Internet Interactive Catalog,* and a global marketplace containing information about products and services."

THE GROOM LAKE DESERT RAT

subscription: psychospy@aol.com

An electronic newsletter for people interested in Area 51, UFOs, government secrecy, and related matters.

GRIST Online

subscription: fowler@phantom.com

"A new journal of electronic network poetry, art and culture. *GRIST* will be eclectic. *GRIST* will be open to all the language and visual art forms that develop on the net."

Holy Temple of Mass Consumption

FTP: quartz.rutgers.edu:/pub/journals/HToMC

"Articles, opinions, reviews, and artwork of a loosely-defined collection of cranks, weirdos, freaks, net personalities, curmudgeons, and anyone else who turns us on at the time. Commentary on nearly everything, with particular attention to societal decay in general and mass-media conspiracy programming in particular."

HotWIRED

subscription: infodroid@wired.com (leave Subject field blank; on line by itself enter: subscribe hotwired)

An online zine from the folks who bring you *Wired*. *HotWIRED* will keep you "informed of current developments with *Wired's* burgeoning online presence—new services, updates, and general stuff we feel net readers of *Wired* will be interested in. This list is not a general-discussion list, but instead will consist of posts from us here in the online department, usually on the order of one every week."

International Teletimes

subscription: editor@teletimes.com (include computer type and country of residence)

"*International Teletimes* is a general interest electronic magazine."

InterText

FTP: etext.archive.umich.edu:/pub/Zines/Literary/InterText

"*InterText* is a free, on-line bi-monthly fiction magazine. It publishes material ranging from mainstream stories to fantasy to horror to science fiction to humor. *InterText* is entering its fourth year of publication; the editors plan to continue publishing *InterText* for the foreseeable future."

"*InterText* publishes in both ASCII/setext (plain text) and PostScript (laser printer) formats, and reaches thousands of readers on six continents worldwide. The ASCII version runs approximately 150K per issue. The PostScript version runs approximately 700K."

Line Noiz

subscription: dodger@fubar.bk.psu.edu (leave Subject field blank; on line by itself enter: subscription linenoiz your-email-address)

"This zine was created to provide a forum for discussion and expression of views and issues related to cyberpunk themes. We wish to allow you to show your own personal views on Cyberpunk and what it means to you. We do not have any restrictions as to who can contribute or receive this zine. You can contribute whether or not you consider yourself a cyberpunk or part of the cyberpunk community (if it exists. That is another question)."

Meta Ezine

FTP: ftp.netcom.com: pub/mlinksva

A monthly electronic zine covering news of interested to the net community: cryptography, privacy, electronic publishing, virtual communities and shareware development.

M. F. O. (Media Foundation Online)

subscription: adbusters@mindlink.bc.ca

"The MEDIA FOUNDATION is a five-year-old commercial-free zone. We are a non-profit society bent on changing the way North Americans live.

"Through television-hijacking, petitions, letter writing campaigns, subvertisements, uncommercials, billboard corrections, monkey-wrenching, networking and pontification, we intend to culture jam the destructive, consumer paradigms that rule our lives in order to save the forests, the air we breathe and the clarity of our own minds."

The Mini-Journal of Irreproducible Results

subscription: listserv@mitvma.mit.edu (leave Subject field blank; on line by itself enter: subscribe mini-jir first-name last-name)

"Publishes news about overly stimulating research and ideas. Specifically: A) Haphazardly selected superficial (but advanced!) extracts of research news and satire from the *Journal of Irreproducible Results* (*JIR*). B) News about the annual Ig Nobel Prize ceremony. Ig Nobel Prizes honor "achievements that cannot or should not be reproduced." A public ceremony is held at MIT, in. Cambridge Massachusetts, every autumn. The ceremony is sponsored jointly by *JIR* and by the MIT Museum. C) News about other science humor activities conducted by the MIT Museum and *JIR*."

The Morpo Review

subscription: morpo-request@morpo.creighton.edu

"How about Sonnets to Captain Kangaroo, free-verse ruminations comparing plastic lawn ornaments to "Love Boat" or nearly anything with cows in it. No, not cute, Smurfy little 'ha ha' ditties—back reality into a corner and snarl! Some good examples are 'Oatmeal' by Galway Kinnell, 'A Supermarket In California' by Allen Ginsberg, or the 6th section of Wallace Stevens' 'Six Significant Landscapes.' "

Obscure Electronic

subscription: obscure@csd4.csd.uwm.edu

"*Obscure* is the zine that profiles the people in this publishing sub-culture."

Phrack Magazine

subscription: phrack@well.sf.ca.us

"An electronic publication covering all facets of the Computer Underground. *Phrack* magazine has been published since 1984 and has grown to become one of the best sources for information about operating systems, bugs, telephony and the world-wide hacker culture."

Practical@narchy

FTP: etext.archive.umich.edu:/pub/politics/spunk

"A bimonthly electronic zine concerning anarchy from a practical point of view, to help you put some anarchy in your everyday life. The anarchy scene is covered through reviews and reports from people in the living anarchy."

Pulse Magazine Electronic Edition

subscription: pulse@drink.demon.co.uk (leave Subject field blank; on line by itself enter: subscribe pulse)

A "monthly magazine for gay men ([the zine is] edited in Scotland)."

RISKS Digest

subscription: listserv@uga.bitnet (in the Subject field enter: sub-scribe risks; in Europe: lindsay.marshall@newcastle.ac.uk)

"Forum on risks to the public in computers and related systems"

Scream Baby

FTP: etext.archive.umich.edu:/pub/zines/cyberpunk/screambaby

"What do I want? Besides world peace, a sexy Mexican maid, and someone to use their fucking brains around here, I want a really good all-encompassing-sub-culture zine. Music, literature, art, television, film, weird space-time kinks, events, information, news, humor, interviews, and reviews of 'Stuff I Think Is Cool.' Not all at once, of course. Each issue of *Scream Baby* will come out whenever I can scrape together 25-30 kilobytes of really good stuff."

TapRoot Reviews Electronic Edition

FTP: etext.archive.umich.edu:/pub/zines/taproot

"Short reviews of micropress poetry, experimental literature and art—100+ reviews per issue."

Terrorist Profile Weekly

subscription: cdibona@mason1.gmu.edu

A round-up of news on terrorists and terrorism, mostly culled from documents at the U.S. Department of State.

• *Japanese Red Army (JRA)*

 aka: Anti-Imperialist International Brigade (AIIB)

 DESCRIPTION

 An international terrorist group formed about 1970 after breaking away from Japanese Communist League Red Army Faction. Now led by Fusako Shigenobu, believed to be in Syrian-garrisoned area of Lebanon's Bekka Valley. Stated goals are to overthrow Japanese Government and monarchy and to help foment world revolution. Organization unclear, but may control or at least have ties to Anti-Imperialist International Brigade (AIIB); may also have links to Antiwar Democratic Front—an overt leftist political organization—inside Japan. Details released following November 1987 arrest of leader Osamu Maruoka indicate that JRA may be organizing cells in Asian cities, such as Manila and Singapore. Has had close and longstanding relations with Palestinian terrorist groups—based and operating outside Japan—since its inception.

The Unplastic News

subscription: tibbetts@hsi.hsi.com

"*The Unplastic News* is a compilation of quotes and stories, all credited to the proper sources and arranged in absolutely no order whatsoever. We present this material for entertainment and for its communication value. Computer networks are a wild form of global human interaction and we hope to post ideas and thoughts to be read and digested."

Voices from the Net

subscription: voices-request@andy.bgsu.edu (in subject: voices from the net, body: subscribe)

"There are a lot of folks with at least one foot in this complex region we call (much too simply) 'the net.' There are a lot of voices on these wires. From IRC to listservs, MUDspace to e-mail, Usenet group to commercial BBS—all kinds of voices—loud and quiet, anonymous and well-known. And yet, it's far from clear what it might mean to be a 'voice' from, or on, the net. Enter *Voices from the Net:* one attempt to sample, explore, the possibilities (or perils) of net voices. Worrying away at the question. Running down the meme. Looking/listening, and reporting back to you."

World Tibet Network News

subscription: wtn-editors@utcc.utoronto.ca

An electronic newsletter from The International Campaign for Tibet, "a Washington-based Tibet monitoring and advocacy group. Established in 1988 as a non-profit organization, ICT promotes human rights and democratic freedoms for Tibetans."

WEIRDNUZ

subscription: notw-request@nine.org

The weekly online version of Chuck Shepherd's *News of the Weird* zine. Shepherd pulls together the best, worst, most ridiculous, and most awful bits of news culled from periodicals from around the world.

- *In September, police in Chiba, Japan, announced the imminent arrests of three men for selling schoolgirls' used underpants in vending machines at a price of about $30 for a set of three. The men are accused of violating the Antique Dealings Act, which regulates the sales of used goods.* [Mainichi Daily News, 9-22-93]

MUSIC

MUSIC

Introduction—Music

The Japanese architect Arata Isozaki has developed a theory of building design which he calls "disjunctive synthesis." Simply, it's his blending of old and new, traditional Japanese rice paper and wood designs with postmodern applications of steel and glass. I like to think that there's a musical variety of disjunctive synthesis. For instance, the two instruments I play most often (when I have time to play at all) are the digital sampler and the didjeridoo. The sampler uses computer disks and a fairly complex MIDI interface that runs direct to a bank of effects, a graphic equalizer and a four-track recorder. The didjeridoo is a big hollow tube into which I can howl or blow a sort of raspberry to make sounds. One instrument wouldn't exist without electricity and microelectronics; the other is acoustic and thousands of years old. I like what each of them can do, and wouldn't want to have to give up either one. When I think about how each of them work, or use the two together, that's disjunctive synthesis. There are more and more people trying to blend these the old and new instruments. A few of them are reviewed in this section (look for Material in the Independent Music section, Steve Roach in New Music and Aisha Kandisha's Jarring Effects in World Music.).

If you think you might like to synthesize some disjunctives of your own, look at the music equipment section in this chapter. We list sources for didjeridoos and acoustic percussion, but also include information on such modern gear as the MidiVox and Emmett Chapman's Stick.

There are also sections on music zines and books. The chapter ends with a listing of music mail order sources. Between the list here and in the first **CCS**, you ought to be able to find just about any album currently in print.

Theremin

information free from: Big Briar, Rt. 3, P.O. Box 115A1, Leicester, NC 28748; voice/fax 704-683-9085

You've heard theremins on everything from old '50s science fiction movie soundtracks to albums by The Beachboys and the Pixies. A theremin is the only instrument you don't touch to play. You play a theremin by moving your hands toward or away from the two antennae on the instrument (one antenna is for pitch, the other for volume). The theremin typically has a 2-1/2 octave range. Synthesizer pioneer Robert Moog has redesigned the instrument for the digital age, making it a more stable instrument and—more exciting—MIDI compatible. A basic theremin from Moog's company, Big Briar, runs from $1800 to $2100.

Didjeridoo

This Australian Aboriginal instrument has gained in popularity in the last few years. It is one of the simplest instruments in the world: a hollow wooden tube that you play something like a giant kazoo. But the sounds you can create are beautiful and unearthly. The following companies all carry didjeridoos (both traditional ones hollowed by termites and new ones carved by hand), instructional tapes, etc. Didjeridoos cost between $200-$600.

Fred Tietjen, 26 Allen St., San Francisco, CA 94109; 415-474-6979; Tietjen also carries "American didjeridoos," made from PVC pipe for $85.

Imlakesh, P.O. Box 8237, Santa Fe, NM, 87504; 505-989-6642

Silver Bush Productions, P.O. Box 541, Forest Knolls, CA 94933; 800-535-7700

The Stick

information free from: Stick Enterprises, 6011 Woodlake Ave., Woodland Hills, CA 91367-3238; 818-884-2001; fax 818-883-0668

Invented by Emmett Chapman, the Stick is sort of a keyboard player's answer to the guitar. You play the Stick by tapping on the strings with the fingers of each hand. The Stick is a popular bass substitute, but experienced players can play both bass, chords and leads. Chapman himself still sells new Sticks, and often has a few reconditioned used ones in stock.

Trey Gunn of Sunday All Over the World plays bass and accompaniment on the Stick. Photo by Ingrid Chavez.

The Multistring Shopper

newsletter free from: Traktor Topaz, 1001 Bridgeway, #216, Sausalito, CA 94965; 415-435-7504

A newsletter for Stick players covering news, techniques, recordings, etc. This is also a good place to find ads for used Sticks.

Voice Controllers

MidiVox

information free from: MidiVox, 1237 Cedar Post Ln., #A3, Houston, TX 77055; 800-433-6434; 713-973-2976; fax 713-973-2721

A professional-quality controller that lets you use your voice to trigger MIDI events. The MidiVox uses mics built into a "biosensor collar" that goes around your throat and senses even subtle vocalizations. The unit is around $2500, and comes with a 2-year warranty.

Casio VA-10

information free from: Casio, 570 Mt. Pleasant Ave., P.O. Box 7000, Dover, NJ 07801; 201-361-5400; fax 201-361-3819

A mid-sized, mid-priced Casio keyboard with a difference: you don't have to play keyboards to use it. By singing through the built-in microphone, you can control any of the 100 synthesized sounds in the VA-10. It's around $200, and not MIDI compatible.

H.E.A.R.

information packet $7 from: Hearing Education and Awareness for Rockers, P.O. Box 460847, San Francisco, CA 94146; 415-773-9590

An information and advocacy group concerned with hearing loss among musicians and how to prevent it. Musicians run the group, and they can recommend hearing protection that lets you hear live music accurately, without damaging your eardrums.

Music Equipment Catalogs

African Percussion

catalog free from: African Percussion, 115 S. Topanga Canyon Blvd., #169, Topanga, CA 90290; 800-733-3786; 818-591-3111

Like the name says—African percussion: drums, bells, gourds, rattles, Balafons, etc. They also carry Brazilian percussion and Australian Aboriginal instruments.

Analogue-Modular Systems

information free from: 213-850-5216; fax 213-850-1059

A clearinghouse for vintage analog synthesizers, from little Minimoogs and Odysseys to massive modular systems. Stock changes constantly, so call with your requests.

Elderly Instruments Catalog

catalog free from: Elderly Instruments, P.O. Box 14210, Lansing, MI 48901-4210; 517-372-7890; fax 517-372-5155

Acoustic instruments and accessories, from the ordinary to the exotic: acoustic and laptop steel guitars, pan pipes, Zydeco rubboards, accordions, talking drums, etc.

Music for Little People

catalog free from: Music for Little People, P.O. Box 1460, Redway, CA 95560; 800-727-2233; fax 707-923-3241

Musical instruments, CDs, cassettes, music education software and videos for kids.

Rogue Music

newsletter free from: Rogue Music, 251 W. 30th St., NY, NY 10001-2801; 212-629-3708; fax 212-947-0027

Used music gear of every type, including recording equipment and computer software. The prices are good (and they take equipment trades) and the staff is knowledgeable. And they're honest—the one time someone screwed up my order, I found a handwritten apology in the box when they sent me the correct gear.

Woodwind & Brasswind Catalog

catalog free from: Woodwind & Brasswind, 19880 State Line Rd., South Bend, IN 46637; 800-348-5003; fax 219-277-2542

The best combo of new gear and prices I've seen. Their *Rock 'n Rhythm* catalog features everything from the latest synths and samplers to guitars, effects, recording gear, stands, lighting equipment, etc. Their *Advanced Technologies* catalog is dedicated to MIDI gear, computer software and hardware, including music educational products.

ZETA MUSIC SYSTEMS

JAZZ VIOLIN

Featuring an ergonomic shape and sleek styling, the Jazz is highly responsive to all playing styles. By removing upper bouts, thinning the body and lowering the string action, Zeta has produced an instrument that facilitates reach to all positions and increases playing speed. Important positional cues such as the headstock heel and an aluminum strut which gives the feel of the upper bout for positional reference have been retained. Available in high gloss black, red and white lacquer finishes. MIDI compatible.

#ZTJV204 4-string .... **Call**
#ZTJV205 5-string .... **Call**

Auron: Musical Tomorrows

$49/6 CDs (CA residents add sales tax) from: Auron, P.O. Box 422248, San Francisco, CA 94142-9858; 800-622-6874

A bimonthly CD compilation of indy musicians that covers a lot of territory. Volume 2, for instance, starts off with a couple of acoustic guitar-powered tunes, the first a complex folk number by Houston's David Rice, and the second a Minsk-based folk band that escaped to the West during a music festival in '88! The rest of the disc is rounded out with some famous names (Mekons, Dave Alvin, Dirty Dozen Brass Band) and many more should-be-famous (Sivuca, Batak, Angels in Heavy Syrup, Kamikaze Ground Crew). From Texas to Japan to New Orleans to Indonesia, the **Auron** sampler series takes you around the world in 70 minutes.

Come Again 2

information from: Silent Records, 101 Townsend, #206, San Francisco, CA 94107; 415-957-1320; fax 415- 957-0779

The word noise means very different things to different people and cultures. In the case of **Come Again 2,** we get a lesson in the Japanese idea of noise. But even in Japan noise means different things to different bands. To Violent Onsen Geisha, noise means a funk groove accompanied by madmen; to Merzbow, noise means a static-riddled blast, like the voice of Satan blasting over shortwave; to Abominable Snowman Effuse Anal Tibet, it means taking a guitar that's playing a simple repetitive figure, like the opening notes of **Twin Peaks**, and torturing the instrument to death.

On **Come Again 2,** nearly two dozen Japanese bands make noise for you, sometimes pleasantly, sometimes hideously, sometimes weirdly. But it's all genuine and relentless. There are no sissies allowed on **Come Again 2.**

Dissemination Network: Transmission 1991-1993

$11 ppd (TX residents add sales tax) from: FringeWare, Inc., P.O. Box 49921, Austin, TX 78765

Language is a virus, and music is a disease vector. Dissemination

Network is dedicated to the spreading of their aural meme throughout culture, or at least your head. Media cut-ups, rhythms like silk jackhammers, keyboards that cut through the net-burn noise and confusion with the precision line of a surgical incision. Dissemination Network wants you to listen. More than that, they want you to be dangerous: they want you to think, and they're willing to techno/hip-hop/rock & roll your Joe Boxers off to do it.

Ethnotechno

TVT Records

Techno, like any technologically-based music, is a prisoner of its form, i.e., since it's generated by machines, anyone who has the right machines thinks that she/he can make music. Wrong. Wrong. Wrong. When you can switch on a machine, and produce a perfect rhythm track every time, imagination (the human factor) becomes very important. **Ethnotechno** is an anthology that shows what machines and smart people can do together. The basic sound is the pure groin-jolting electronic pulse that made techno popular in the first place, but on top of that, you have layers of sound sources such as traditional Japanese music, Yoruban ceremonial vocals, American Shawnee Indians, Algerian singers, Burmese drummers...The mixture of old and new on **Ethnotechno** is the kind of kick techno needs now. I can't wait to see where it goes next.

Brian Gingrich: Anxious Days and Forty Nights

$14 ppd from: Brian Gingrich, 5301 S. Rockwell, Chicago, IL 60632; 312-778-3912

Space shuttle soundtracks for earth-gazing. Storm clouds, the broad African savannahs, icebergs breaking up along the arctic coast; ash plumes knot from the mouths of active volcanoes. Somewhere below, shore birds are feeding where the Amazon meets the Atlantic.

The Robert Fripp String Quintet: The Bridge Between

The California Guitar Trio: Yamanashi Blues

Trey Gunn: One Thousand Years

information free from: Possible Productions, 351 Magnolia Ave., Long Beach, CA 90802; voice/fax 310-491-1945

Ever since he started teaching his Guitar Craft workshops, Robert Fripp has made it a point to record with his students. Some of these recordings have sounded a lot like what they were: clever students playing difficult exercises well.

Time has passed, and the workshops have been around long enough to spawn spin-off bands, one of which, The Robert Fripp String Quintet, is really the blending of two bands. Consisting of Fripp and Trey Gunn from Sunday All Over The World, and Bert Lams, Paul Richards and Hideyo Moriya of The California Guitar Trio, this group succeeds where Fripp's other Guitar Craft-based bands fail. Part of the answer lies in the composition chores. This isn't the Robert Fripp show. A number of the tunes the quintet plays are reworkings of compositions by and for The California Guitar Trio. Trey Gunn is also a commanding arranger and player. This is perhaps the first post-King Crimson recording that never feels like Robert Fripp and a Bunch of Other Guys.

Yamanashi Blues, by The California Guitar Trio, is named for member Bert Lams' thoughtful and introspective piece that opens the disc. Their technique and sound is flawless, and they sound as if they genuinely enjoy playing with each other. And, despite their name, the trio doesn't take itself too seriously. The tunes on **Yamanashi Blues** range from originals to a Bach fugue to an acoustic reworking of the old Ventures hit, "Walk Don't Run."

In contrast with the previous two albums, the sound of Trey Gunn's **One Thousand Years** is very electric, based around Gunn's Stick which he uses to create both bass and sinewy guitar leads. While Gunn's voice is nothing remarkable, his compositions are complex, subdued structures, full of tension and beautifully layered lines of treated Stick.

Possible Productions also has a video of The Robert Fripp String Quintet live in Japan. For collectors, all of the CDs are available in special autographed editions.

Jon Hassell and Bluescreen: Dressing for Pleasure

Warner Bros.

On **Dressing for Pleasure**, Jon Hassell has reconstructed hip-hop in his own image. Working with players from bands as diverse as Tom Waits' and Miles Davis', as well as programmer/sample-master BLK Lion, Hassell takes hip-hop's idea of assembling new tunes from stripped down samples of pop, jazz and funk and has expanded the mix to include styles and techniques from the whole world. The result is like dance music for a virtual club, hacked together by refugees from some pan-global sound crew for whom national borders and rules about what instrument goes with what simply don't apply.

Anton LaVey: Strange Music

$10 ppd ($11 Canada/Mexico; $13 overseas; make check payable to "Gregg Turkington") from: Amarillo Records, P.O. Box 24433, San Francisco, CA 94124

He's partied with politicos and movie stars like Jayne Mansfield. He's kept a pet lion in his basement. He's the biggest name in the Satan biz. He's Anton LaVey, the guy whose shaven head and spooky goatee has graced many a Satanists-live-among-us scare story in the tabloids. What many people don't know is that in his younger, pre-Satanic adman days, LaVey played keyboards in carnivals, circuses and strip shows. And he's kept up his chops. **Strange Music** has LaVey cakewalking through such instrumental standards as "One for My Baby (And One More for the Road)," "Temptation," "Thanks for the Memory" (yes, Bob Hope's favorite song), as well as such obscure gems as "Gloomy Sunday," billed "as probably the world's champion suicide song." **Strange Music** is a must-have for all adventurous music lovers. Even if you're going to burn in Hell for buying it.

Dr. John: Mos' Scocious

$30.98 ppd (CA residents add sales tax) from: Rhino Records, 10635 Santa Monica Blvd., LA, CA 90025; 800-432-0020

There's no better introduction to modern New Orleans music than this 2-disc set covering the entire career of Mac Rabennack, aka Dr. John. From the early (and mostly obscure) recordings like "Bad Neighborhood" by Ronnie & The Delinquents, which mixes '50s vocal harmonies with New Orleans swing, "Storm Warning" (on which Dr. John plays guitar, his first instrument), through his mid-'70s hit, "Right Place Wrong Time," and on to his recent recordings, you hear the streets of New Orleans changing around you, absorbing new influences and new styles, but always remaining essentially New Orleans. There's over 2 hours of music on **Mos' Scocious**, 39 songs, and not a dud in the bunch.

Also recommended: **Going Back to New Orleans**

Material: Hallucination Engine

Axiom/Island

Bill Laswell is a musical chameleon. Always restless, always experimenting, he also has the kind of chops and credibility that means when he wants to put together a band, or try out an idea, he can call in some big guns to help out. In this incarnation of the band Material, you can find downtown, jazz and funk luminaries such as Wayne Shorter, Bernie Worrell, Bootsy Collins, and Sly Dunbar, as well as world music heavyweights, Shankar, Simon Saheen, Liu Sola, Zakir Hussain, and Trilok Gurtu. Though it's just a temporary arrangement, Material sounds like a band that's been together for years. **Hallucination Engine** is an opium-laced stroll through a strange country whose customs are familiar, yet remain enigmatic, whose architecture reminds you of both ancient Persia and the Mongol Empire, whose smells are as exotic as the rarest spice, and earthy as horseshit in the gutters.

Also recommended: **Seven Souls; Praxis: Sacrifist; Death Cube K: Dreamatorium**

The Outer Limits

information free from: Crescendo Record Co., 8400 Sunset Blvd., Hollywood, CA 90069; 213-656-2614

Anyone who watched **The Outer Limits** as a kid remembers that the sound of the thing was as frightening as the images on the TV screen. This was due mostly to the composing talent of Dominic Frontiere, who provided the atmospheric background music for the show. This CD brings together three suites Frontiere wrote for three different **Outer Limits** episodes. While originally recorded in state-of-the-art low-fi, the music itself remains potent and unnerving.

RE/Search: Incredibly Strange Music, Volume 1

$16 CD; $13.99 ppd each (CA residents add sales tax) from: RE/Search, 20 Romolo St., Ste. B, San Francisco, CA 94133

Modern science and culture has produced many mutants—from the ten-eyed trout near Chernobyl to the twisted musics found in department store cut-out bins. **Incredibly Strange Music** is sort of a primer for this nearly lost musical kitsch culture. You can hear early synthesizer abominations such as "Swan's Splashdown," a painfully dissonant sitar version of "Up, Up & Away," Fred Lowry's virtuoso whistling of the William Tell Overture, as well as inhumanly fast versions of "Tico Tico" and "Flight of the Bumblebee." For all its silliness, the music is quite entertaining because there isn't a smug or self-conscious moment on the disc.

Shinjuku Thief: Bloody Tourist

information from: Darkwave, P.O. Box 1591, Garden Grove, CA 92642-1591; 818-395-7699; fax 818-395-7697

Thieves survive by their wits, by moving fast, and by making the best use of whatever they can get their hands on. Shinjuku Thief uses synths, guitars, sound samples, and acoustic exotica such as the *shakuhachi* flute for source material. Their sound ranges from the heavy metal rush of "Komachi Ruins" to the sparse and brittle "Preacher's Ghost." Shinjuku Thief is a band that hangs out at the crossroads where the past and the future meet.

John Adams: Hoodoo Zephyr

Elektra Nonesuch

This album must have been a relief for Adams to make. Best known for two major modern operas, **Nixon in China** and **The Death of Klinghoffer,** Adams takes a giant step back from big casts, lighting worries, budget problems and deadlines. **Hoodoo Zephyr** is a solo project, just Adams and a bunch of synthesizers. There are seven cuts here, songs with unsung lyrics that center around landscape and travel. The lyrics are included with the disc, so you can try to sing along or just forget them, enjoying Adams' lovely melodies and playing for themselves.

Also Recommended: **The Chairman Dances; Shaker Loops/ Phrygian Gates; Light over Water; The Wound Dresser**

Robert Ashley: Private Parts (The Record)

Lovely Music

A combination of subtle keyboards, tabla and voice form the basis for the opening section of Ashley's enormous "opera" cycle. Ashley's own tranquilized voice reads the text: a stream-of-consciousness portrait of movement, of personal travel and change. All the while, the sounds of violin-like synthesizer, piano and tabla drift through the background, like clouds scudding across the horizon. **Private Parts** is a very modern and intimate work that will grab you immediately or have you diving for the "off" switch.

Copernicus: No Borderline

for information, send SASE to: Nevermore, Inc., P.O. Box 170150, Brooklyn, NY 11217

If he'd been born a few hundred years ago, Copernicus would have been burned as a witch; if he'd been born two thousand years ago, no doubt he would have been a successful prophet, with minions and disciples all his own. He'd probably have ended up crucified.

Copernicus is a musical ringmaster, an orator of tremendous power who chants, recites and screams his blank verse over complex musical figures provided by his band. There is a Book of Revelations quality to this. Copernicus' imagery extends from the atomic world to the whole universe. He crushes it, shrieks at it, and remakes it in his own image, and manages to make it all an enthralling listen. St. John crossed with Kurt Weill.

Alvin Curran: Songs and Views of the Magnetic Garden

BMG Classics

A haunting work that combines natural and synthesized sounds into a mysterious environment of rare colors and forms. Curran's sound palette ranges from the simplest to some of the highest-tech available in the mid-'70s (when the piece was first recorded). Traces of wind, the sound of swallows and high-tension wires, whirled tubes, frogs, and other real-world sounds are treated and woven together with the tones from glass chimes, synthesizers, kalimba, ring modulator and percussion. This could be the soundtrack for a Max Ernst landscape.

Tom Djill: Mutootator

$12 ($13 foreign) ppd from: Soul on Rice Productions, 2312 Spaulding Ave., Berkeley, CA 94703-1628; 510-848-3305

Bay Area improv masters get together to play and rough up each other's aesthetics with guitars, cellos, saxes, synths, and homemade percussion. Sometimes the improvised riffs get sampled and replayed, instantly adding another player or small ensemble to the group that's already slashing away. The effect is jarring and intriguing, moving from airhorn-in-your-ear-loudness to a kind of neurotic *pianissimo,* from sonorous marimba runs to the *sckrechh!* of something scraping the inside of your skull clean.

Ellen Fullman: Body Music

information from: Experimental Intermedia, 224 Centre Street, New York, NY 10013

Fullman has developed a whole musical language based on her "long-stringed instrument." The instrument is simply a series of wires running between two large wooden boxes that act as resonators. By rubbing or striking the wires at points between the resonators, Fullman and her ensemble set up complex, overlapping tones and overtones, similar at times to the drone of a church organ or the sound of a sitar. This is hypnotic stuff, the drone of metallic insects hunting for machine oil and honey.

I Wayan Sadra: Karya

New Music from Indonesia, Vol. 3

$19.98 ppd (NY residents add sales tax) from: Lyrichord Discs, 141 Perry Street, New York, NY 10014; 212-929-8234

Indonesian composer I Wayan Sadra has emerged as one of the most distinctive voices in new music, combining traditional music forms and instruments from Java, Bali, Sunda, Sumatra and the U.S. with a compositional style influenced both by Sadra's study of traditional Indonesian styles and his experimental bent. What emerges is a new sound, rooted in the folk sounds and forms of his home, but working out in new directions, bringing Indonesian music up to a level equal with local dance (where in the past, music has been secondary). **Karya** is required listening for fans of gamelan and new music alike.

Also recommended: **Asmat Dream; Mana 689**

Music for 3 Pianos

Gyroscope/Caroline

Ruben Garcia: Colors in Motion

information from: Close Tolerance Music, P.O. Box 1964, Joshua Tree, CA 92252; 619-366-3820; fax 619-366-3149

Six short pieces recorded in a single day by three prominent new music pianists: Harold Budd, Ruben Garcia, and Daniel Lentz. The compositions are simple, spare, and engaging. There are no egos here, no jostling for solos. This is the sound of musicians who listen as well as they play.

Ruben Garcia's independent solo album, **Colors in Motion,** is a more complex affair, mixing synthesized percussion and melodies with piano tones. Even with the more complex instrumentation, Garcia's music remains simple and uncluttered. The individual pieces are quite pretty, structured more for a lyrical quality than compositional or technical flash.

Newband: Play Microtonal Works

information from: Mode Records, P.O. Box 375, Kew Gardens, NY 11415

For some composers there just aren't enough notes in the standard equal- or well-tempered scale systems. So they invent their own "microtonal" scales, using intervals smaller than the standard scales.

Harry Partch worked out a 43-note scale system, and invented instruments to make full use of it. He's represented on this disc with the surprisingly consonant, "Two Studies on Ancient Greek Scales," which features the flute and the "zoomoozophone," an instrument invented by his assistant Dean Drummond (who has two strong pieces on the disc). John Cage also worked with microtonal scales, and contributes his own flute/zoomoozophone duet. The remaining piece is by Joan LaBarbara, who is known more as a singer of 20th-century works than as a composer. Her piece is fine, subtle and easy on the ears.

Michael Nyman: The Piano

Virgin

Much of composer Michael Nyman's best work has been for movies. His music for Jane Campion's *The Piano* serves a number of roles. First, it has to express the inner life of Holly Hunter's mute heroine. For this, Nyman wove together simple Scottish folk melodies. He also had to create the incidental music that would underpin the film. For this, he uses a full orchestra, arranging and conducting his own lush scores. The resulting music is both gorgeous and moving.

Open Space, Vols. 1-5

information from: Open Space, R.D. 2, Box 45E, Red Hook, NY 12571

The Open Space series presents old and new experimental music in clean recordings on CD. Some of the oldest pieces (Benjamin Boertz's "Group Variations for Computer" on Volume 5) go back to the late '60s. Boertz's piano work from the '80s is well-represented on the four-disc second volume of the series, "8 Piansolo Soundsessions." Volume 1 also contains two long piano works, while Volume 3 features experiments with voices and text. By digitally recording these early and experimental works, Open Space is guaranteeing that they won't be lost or forgotten.

Arvo Pärt: Tabula Rasa

ECM New Series

A set of outstanding small ensemble pieces. First released in the mid-'80s, these cyclical compositions exist under the hushed influence of the Eastern Orthodox church, a religious body with a more internal, almost Buddhist, view of spirituality than the Roman church. Unlike much modern music, Pärt's ensemble works—for violin and piano, string orchestra, 12 cellos, violin and prepared piano—form a kind of solid, spiritual whole.

Also recommended: **Te Deum**

Steve Roach: Dreamtime Return

$31.48 ppd (CA residents add sales tax) from: Backroads, 417 Tamal Plaza, Corte Madera, CA 94925; 800-825-4848

Steve Roach is one of the few synthesizer players around who has been able to move between a rock-oriented Tangerine Dream-type sound and a more expansive, experimental vision. It's these qualities that make **Dreamtime Return** his finest work. Moving from purely synthesized tones, he brings in sound sources such as the didjeridoo, frame drum, rainstick, and Aboriginal singing to create a portrait of the Australian Outback. Pieces such as "Airtribe Meets the Dream Ghost" and "Red Twilight with the Old Ones" use these disparate sonic combinations to achieve a spacious, memorable sound.

Tibetan Singing Bowl Ensemble: Nightsongs

information from: Scarlet Records/Infinity, 605 Ridgefield Rd., Wilton CT, 06897-1625; 203-762-2102

The motto of the Tibetan Singing Bowl Ensemble is "New Music for Old Instruments." Originally using only brass singing bowls (which the players rubbed or struck with wooden mallets), they've expanded their sound base to include clay flutes, Tibetan thighbone trumpet, didjeridoo, *shofar* (a ram's horn), jaw harp, and other unusual acoustic instruments. The ensemble performs all their music live, with no dubs or effects. All the strange tones and overtones you hear are from simple acoustic instruments played by real people. **Nightsongs** conjures up exotic soundscapes like no others you've heard.

Hector Zazou: Sahara Blue

TriStar Music

Back in the '70s, record companies liked to put together what they called "supersessions," where they got all the most famous rock guitarists, drummers, bass players, and singers around, stuck them in a studio and let them musically duke it out. **Sahara Blue** has a little bit of that "supersession" feel to it, but unlike most of those ersatz rock bands, this group works because, ultimately, it's all under the control of one person: Hector Zazou. Zazou's previous releases have included pieces for synthesizers and small ensembles, in styles from the simple to the stentorian. **Sahara Blue** is a collection of songs and tone poems based on the poetry of Arthur Rimbaud. It brings together an odd assortment of talents: Gérard Depardieu, John Cale, Khaled, Bill Laswell, Ryuchi Sakamoto, Keith Leblanc, David Sylvian, etc. Highly romantic and dramatic, the breathy recitations and often languid music of **Sahara Blue** could make it a Barry White-type seduction album for new music fans.

based on Arthur Rimbaud's poems, SAHARA BLUE is *directed by* Hector ZAZOU The music was played by the SAHARA BLUE Orchestra *starring* John Cale, Gérard Depardieu, Khaled, Annel Drecker, Dominique Dalcan, Bill Laswell, Tim Simenon, Barbara Louise Cogan *and*.

Africa: Never Stand Still

CD $47.45; cassette $32.45 ppd each (NY residents add sales tax) from: Ellipsis Arts, 20 Lumber Road, Roslyn, NY 11576; 800-788-6670

This 3-disc set from Ellipsis Arts is one of the best introductions to African popular music I've ever heard. It covers so many countries and styles, it's hard to know where to begin. There are some names that will be familiar to anyone interested in African pop: Ladysmith Black Mambazo, Youssou N'Dour, Remmy Ongala, Baaba Maal, and Ali Farka Toure. But there are dozens of other excellent performers you might never have heard of: the soukous Singer Pepe Kalle, the percussion ensemble Farafina, Nigerian juju singer Sir Shina Peters, Zimbabwean music innovator, Thomas Mapfumo, and many, many others. A 48-page color booklet accompanies the set, giving you photos and the background of each artist, both as an individual performer and within his or her culture.

Ashkabad: City of Love

Real World

Somehow, in the West we've gotten the idea that love songs have to be slow, serious tunes with way too many violins. Fortunately, straight outta the Russian Republic of Turkmenistan comes Ashkabad. Their name means "City of Love," and they're here to kick down your apartment walls and bust up your romance. Imagine the coolest belly-dancing band in the world, toss in a hint of Western jazz, Middle Eastern seasonings, and songs about love lost and gained. Ashkabad's tempos are seldom what we would consider laid back, but they're always sensuous, as in the instrumental "Gassan." More typical, though, is the frenetic pace of love songs such as "Bibining" and "Kethshpelek." Ashkabad gives us a glimpse of a very different way of musical seduction—not through turgid ballads, but through joyful and exhausting exuberance.

Bunggridj-bunggridj: Wangga Songs by Alan Maralung

$16 ppd (MD residents add sales tax) from: Smithsonian/Folkways, 416 Hungerford Dr., #320, Rockville, MD 20850; 301-443-2314

Traditional didjeridoo and vocal music from Northern Australia. This is the voice of the earth—grinding, growling, shouting—giving birth to land, the animals, and humans. The sound of the Earth before humans had invented "time." A 44-page booklet accompanies the disc, explaining the individual songs, and giving you some background on Australian Aboriginal music.

Djivan Gasparyan: Moon Shines at Night

Gyroscope/Caroline

The *duduk* is a Middle Eastern wind instrument with a sinuous, mournful, almost vocal sound. It's probably the saddest sounding instrument in the world. With the *duduk*, Djivan Gasparyan paints pictures of desert landscapes under the moon, half-collapsed shrines and temples swallowed up by the sand. Lovers used to meet there at night, centuries ago. Now their bodies are one with the hot dust that blows all night and day across the dunes.

Global Meditation

Global Celebration

CD $47.45; cassette $32.45 ppd each from: Ellipsis Arts, 20 Lumber Road, Roslyn, NY 11576; 800-788-6670

What is packaged like a dopey New Age music soporific is, in reality, a tour of meditative and spiritual music from around the world. The set is divided into four discs, each covering a different aspect of sound and song: Songs & Chants, Ensembles, Rhythm & Percussion, and Melody. The variety of sound and styles on any single disc is remarkable. On the first disc alone, you can listen to contemplative music from places like Norway, Bali, Hawaii, Gabon, Japan, England, Tibet, Algeria, and Russia.

If you like **Global Meditation,** you might also want to ignore the packaging of another multi-disc set from the same company. **Global Celebration** is a "best-of" collection from festivals around the world. You can hear the Master Musicians of Jajouka, Hopi Indian dances, Irish reels, a New Orleans Mardi Gras band, an American Baptist choir, Tahitian chants, Malagasy zithers, Cuban Santeria musicians, and on and on. A perfect set for a restless music lover.

Sol Hoopii: Master of the Hawaiian Guitar, Vol. I

information from: Rounder Records, One Camp Street, Cambridge, MA 02140; 617-354-0700; fax 617-491-1970

You take a simple instrument like the guitar and drop it in a new culture and you never know what you'll get back. In the case of Hawaii, we got back a retuned instrument that sounded sort of like the guitar we once knew, but there was something new and weird about it. The Hawaiians retuned the thing all sorts of ways, but mostly they tuned it down, which loosened the strings (hence the generic name "slack key guitar"). Sol Hoopii was the first recording king of Hawaiian steel guitar. His jazz playing is clean and creative, and his use of the slide makes the instrument sound like one big snake, humming contentedly after a swell meal. These early Sol Hoopii tracks were recorded between 1926 and 1930, so the sound quality varies wildly from song to song, but when you get a real master at the top of his game, what's a few scratches and pops?

Huun-Huur-Tu: 60 Horses in My Herd

CD $14.80; cassette $9.80 ppd ea (NJ residents add sales tax) from: Shanachie Records, 37 E. Clinton St., Newton, NJ 07860; 201-579-7763

Centuries ago, the Mongolian tribes that roamed from China up through eastern Russia developed a form of singing often called "mouth music." It uses the same technique that Tibetan monks use to chant several notes at once—throat and breath control forces the singer's voice up into his skull; by controlling his breath and the shape of his mouth and throat, the singer can create an amazing array of harmonies which often contain inhumanly high and low notes.

Huun-Huur-Tu is band from Tuva, a region in southern Siberia. On **60 Horses in My Herd** they mix their extended vocals with guitar, bells, conch shells and the banjo-like *doshpuluur*, creating a sound as haunting, enigmatic, and distant as the windy Tuvan steppes.

Aisha Kandisha's Jarring Effects: Shabeesation

information from: Stern's, 598 Broadway, NY, NY 10012; 212-925-

1648; fax 212-925-1689

A manic hip-hop/funk/dub party in Tangiers and downtown New York. LPs scratch and synths whine while violins, voices and traditional Middle Eastern instruments twist their way through the sonic melee. Sufi ecstasy meets urban American heat. The body and the soul are one.

Juan Pena Lebrijano & Orquestra Andalusi De Tanger

information from: Round World Music, 593 Guerrero, San Francisco, CA 94110; 415-255-8411; mail order 415-255-7384

In the 15th century, the Spanish Inquisition tossed the Muslims (and Jews) out of Spain, hoping to create a purely Christian, European state. Of course, it failed miserably. Aside from the influence that came through constant trade with North Africa, the art of Islam had left an indelible mark on the Iberian peninsula. This disc is proof enough of that, pairing a Spanish Flamenco vocalist with a Moroccan instrumental group. Their dramatic and highly romantic styles mesh perfectly, with Flamenco handclaps bouncing off the dark harmonies of *oud* riffs, all of it floating atop massed female backup vocals. Sorry Torquemada. You never stood a chance.

Mbuti Pygmies of the Huri Rainforest

$16 ppd (MD residents add sales tax) from: Smithsonian/Folkways, 416 Hungerford Dr., #320, Rockville, MD 20850; 301-443-2314

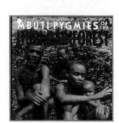

If you've heard 1992's surprise hit album, **Deep Forest,** you've already heard the sound of pygmy songs, though electronically sampled, altered and looped. If you want to hear the unadulterated thing, try **Mbuti Pygmies of the Huri Rainforest,** a series of original field recordings from 1957-58. The chants on this disc are rhythmic and hypnotic, full of overlapping voices chanting in a complex call-and-response pattern. Whether chanting in groups, singing alone, or accompanied by a *mbira* (kalimba), these voices move sweetly and surely through the air.

Ayub Ogada: En Mana Kuoyo

Real World

On **En Mana Kuoyo,** Kenyan Ayub Ogada performs folk and original tunes mixing guitar and organ with traditional percussion and flutes. The tunes are lovely, mostly laid-back affairs, full of plucked strings (from Ogada's lute-like *nyatiti*) and tight harmonies. **En Mana Kuoyo** goes way beyond exotic appeal. This is an album to give anyone who's afraid that African music might be too alien for them.

Lauren Pomerantz: Wings of Time

$19.48 ppd (CA residents add sales tax) from: Musical Offering, 2430 Bancroft Way, Berkeley, CA 94704; 800-466-0211

While **Juan Pena Lebrijano & Orquestra Andalusi De Tanger** (see page 109) gives you a taste of the Muslim influence on Spanish music, **Wings of Time** demonstrates the Jewish influence. These are the songs of the Sephardim, Jews who lived in medieval Spain and Portugal. The songs here concern then-contemporary Jewish lives and folklore; there are secular as well as religious tunes. Above the familiar medieval sound of contrapuntal flute, guitar, and drum soars Lauren Pomerantz's voice. She has a clear affection for the music, and the skill to deliver the melodies with passion.

Calypso Rose: Soca Diva
Superblue: Flag Party

information from: Round World Music, 593 Guerrero, San Francisco, CA 94110; 415-255-7384

A party for your ears and hips. Salsa-spiced horns, Caribbean rhythms and Calypso Rose's voice collide head-on and set off fireworks like New Year's Eve and the Fourth of July all rolled into one.

No less exuberant than Calypso Rose, Superblue is a calypso iconoclast. Coming from the tradition of brass band competitions in Trinidad and Tobago, Superblue keeps blowing away (and pissing off) the old guard "real calypso" purists by penning brass marches that defy easy categorization. Let's just say, if you've never marched to a march in your life, you'd march to these. And dance, too!

Sola: Blues in the East

Axiom/Island

Liu Sola is a traditional Chinese vocalist who left her homeland when she heard the blues. Those scales and bending notes in traditional blues recordings sounded familiar enough to her that she wanted to explore that new terrain, but was informed by her music bosses that American blues were ideologically incorrect. So, like any good blues player, she hit the road. Fastforward to New York, and enter Bill Laswell. He put Sola in the studio with a pack of the best NY jazz and experimental music sidemen, along with *shakuhachi* players and Wu Man, another Chinese instrumentalist who squeezes blues-like bends out of her mandolin-like *pipa*.

Värtinnä: Seleniko

$18 ppd from: Green Linnet Records, 43 Beaver Brook Rd., Danbury, CT 06810; 203-730-0333; fax 203-730-0345

This is a lively recording of Finnish folk tunes—mostly about love and marriage—by an acoustic band with four strong female singers. Though the music is from Finland, you'll find a lot that's familiar here: the rhythms are reminiscent of Irish jigs and the tight, soaring vocal lines resonate in Asian and Middle Eastern modes.

What is Bhangra?

information from: IRS Merchandising, P.O. Box 4346, N. Hollywood, CA 91617; 800-336-2477; 818-508-4253

Anyone who's heard the soundtrack from an Indian movie knows that Hindi musicians have a magpie view of sound. They'll lift any appealing riff or style and work it into the mix. Although it's more technologically sophisticated than most Indian music, Bhangra is no exception when it comes to gene-splicing Western and Indian styles to form a weird, new hybrid organism. At its heart, Bhangra is dance club music. Indian hip-hop. In fact, hip-hop is one of the most obvious styles you'll hear in a Bhangra set, along with traces of rap, techno, disco and, to a lesser extent, rock. Bhangra may be old news in London, but it's kept a fairly low profile in America. A sampler of 13 hot dance tunes by nine bands, **What is Bhangra?** might just be the album to turn that around.

Voices of Forgotten Worlds

Traditional Music of Indigenous People

ed. by Larry Blumenfield

1993; 96 pp.
book w/CDs $37.45; w/cassettes $32.45 ppd each (NY residents add sales tax) from: Ellipsis Arts, 20 Lumber Road, Roslyn, NY 11576; 800-788-6670

A book and recording combination that will introduce you to the music and worlds of 28 indigenous groups around the globe. The beautifully illustrated book explains, simply and briefly, the background and social systems of the groups, and the accompanying double-CDs or cassettes let you hear their voices. You'll see and hear indigenous people from three American Indian tribes, as well as Solomon Islanders, Inuits, Tibetans, Maoris, Ladakhis, Mayans, Kanaks, Bataks and more. Two hours of music in all.

Queering the Pitch

The New Gay & Lesbian Musicology

ed. by P. Brett, E. Wood, G. Thomas

$16.95; Routledge
1994; 320 pp.

A group of lesbian and gay musicologists, academics, performers, and critics take look at the history of western classical music with an unapologetically political eye. The book poses questions such as "Is music the patriarchy's most powerful weapon in constructing and controlling sexual roles?" and "If you scratch an opera queen, will you find a lesbian?" The book also gives queer interpretation to some famous musical works, and looks at the lives of some modern gay composers.

Zouk

World Music in the West Indies

by Jocelyne Guilbault

$24.95; University of Chicago Press
1993; 279 pp.

A thorough, if occasionally academic, look at the history, lyrics, structure, choreography, and social milieu of the infectious dance music called "zouk." The book is illustrated with photos of zouk stars, as well as transcriptions of songs and translations of lyrics. There is also a 48-minute CD with the book, which makes the book a bargain at around $25.

Elevator Music

A Surreal History Of Muzak, Easy-Listening and Other Moodsong

by Joseph Lanza

$22; St. Martin's Press
1994; 280 pp.

Muzak, like all the marvels of the mechanical age, is a two-edged sword. Background music can enhance environments, make them more interesting (an art gallery or restaurant) and less threatening (a doctor's office or airplane). But background music can also influence behavior, speeding up and slowing down your thinking processes, suppressing or stimulating your mood, etc. Offices have used background music for years as a way to keep workers more productive. In 1973, the National Stockyards discovered that Muzak calmed cattle and made them easier to slaughter. In the '70s, background music in public became so ubiquitous that the U.N. passed a resolution confirming individuals' right to silence!

This history of Muzak, million-string easy-listening discs, ambient, and movie music is another in a series of books that reveals secret histories of the modern world. It's required reading for anyone alive and in possession of ears.

- *The 101 Strings managed to reproduce America as it might be seen through the eyes of touring foreigners. Their music elicits a feeling akin to the one we experience when watching German tourists visiting the micro-Bavaria at Busch Gardens. The world America thought it had conquered and flattered through imitation flatters it back with French intellectuals deconstructing the cowboy, Japanese entertainers impersonating Vegas lounge singers, or Saudi Arabian and Indian adventure movies that ape American culture but never get it quite right, since they lack the precise intricacies of dress, gesture, and language to which we cling for identity.*

Ragopedia

by Shiv Dayal Batish & Ashwin Batish

1992; 80 pp.
$37.50 ppd (CA residents add sales tax) from: Batish Publications, 1310 Mission St., Santa Cruz, CA 95060; 408-423-1699

An encyclopedia of North Indian Raga scales written in both Indian *sargam* and Western notation. The Ragopedia covers basic theory and references 680 of the most popular north Indian Ragas.

Incredibly Strange Music, Vol. 2

ed. by Andrea Juno & V. Vale

1994; 220 pp.
$21.99 ppd (CA residents add sales tax) from: RE/Search, 20 Romolo St., Ste. B, San Francisco, CA 94133; 415-362-1465

A deeper, weirder look into the world of musical exotica, obscurity, and madness. Check out the record collections of collectors, performers and stars: Jello Biafra, Korla Pandit, Robert Moog, Ken Nordine, Yma Sumac, Bebe Barron (of the Barrons who performed the soundtrack for *Forbidden Planet*). Heavily illustrated with vintage album covers. An education, a travelogue and a cultural history lesson all in one!

Meet the Residents

by Ian Shirley

1993; 191 pp.
$25.50 ppd from: SeeHear, 59 E. 7th St., NY, NY 10003; 212-982-6968; fax 212-387-8017; in UK: Wings Mail Order, 071-704-7063

The Author's Note that opens the book and the first paragraph of the chapter "The Early Years" alone tells you a lot about the Residents. Both the Note and the chapter opening refer to lies, subjective viewpoints, and best-guesses. Even after twenty years of musical marauding, the Residents remain a mystery. Who the hell are they? How many of them are there? Where are they from? Why do they do all that weird stuff they do? And what's the deal with the eyeballs? Author Ian Shirley tries to find out, and fill in the band's history, and does as good a job as any outsider can. Of course, he could be another ringer in the Residents' ceaseless plot to keep their identities and origins secret!

The Ice Opinion

by Ice T and Heidi Siegmund
$17.95; St. Martin's Press
1994; 199 pp.

We've lost an important option in this country. We've gotten the idea that in order to like or respect someone we have to agree with *everything* that person says. Honest disagreement among friends and allies is not permitted. That's too bad, because when we cut ourselves off from each others' point of view, we miss a lot. Ice T is a guy with opinions about virtually everything: cops, the government, drugs, money, women, men, music, sex, language, religion, racism, crime...etc. He's a smart guy; he's a voice to be heard. Will you agree with everything in his book? Probably not, the same way Ice won't agree with everything you have to say. Should that stop you (us) from reading it? Hell no. If we don't listen to each other, we remain strangers—isolated—and no one gets anywhere. Read this book. Get happy or get pissed off. Whatever. Just don't stop listening to other voices.

• *The most peaceful time I ever experienced in South Central was during the riots. While everybody was looking for fires, we walked through the streets. Kids were setting shit on fire, people were smiling. Everybody was shaking each other's hands, feeling a camaraderie. It was as if the people had taken the city back. For those few days, it belonged to us and it was peaceful....When I drove back into Hollywood, I ran into members of Queer Nation, and they were fucking shit up. I started rolling with the Nation while they were yelling, "Fuck the police." It was the wildest shit in the world.*

What you saw on TV was not what it was. There were white people downtown at Parker Center tearing shit up, too. There were even white people in the middle of South Central protesting and helping in any way they could. They were taken right into the community. There were no stories about that.

8-Track Mind

$8/year (4 issues; make checks payable to "Russel Forster") from: 8-TM Publications, P.O. Box 90, E. Detroit, MI 48021-0090

The social history and cultural significance of the 8-track tape is examined in astonishing and quirky detail.

Ben is Dead

$20/6 issues (Canada $35; overseas $45) from: Ben is Dead, P.O. Box 3166, Hollywood, CA 90028

Extremely smart and funny L.A.-based music and culture zine. Each issue has a theme: sex, information overload, revenge, censorship, etc. Interviews, reviews, killer ads.

Fond Affexxions

$20/year (4 issues) from: Fond Affexxions, 6312 E. Santa Ana Canyon Rd., #112, Anaheim Hills, CA 92807

Attention to production values—both in design and prose—make this a zine to look out for. The music they cover is progressive and industrial pop: Love Spirals Downwards, Paul Westerberg, Bill Nelson, etc. Nice paper. Nice art. Nice zine.

Goldmine

$22/13 issues from: Goldmine, 700 E. State St., Iola, WI 54990; 715-445-2214; fax 715-445-4087

For vinyl and CD collectors. The zine is mostly ads for vintage and rare recordings, with a few articles tossed in.

MIDI

$19.95/year (8 issues; Canada/Mexico $31.95; overseas $39.95) from: Midi Magazine, P.O. Box 6100, Holliston, MA 01746-6100

Interviews with tech-based musicians, and MIDI how-to articles. Hardware and software reviews. Informative and attractive, too.

The Probe

information from: Aaron Muentz, P.O. Box 5068, Pleasanton, CA 94566; 510-278-9946

Alternative rock zine that's smart and sexy. Number 3 has interviews with Lisa Suckdog, All You Can Eat's Japanese tour diary, major label slamming, and loads of reviews.

Ruckus

information from: Comet McKinney, 3712 N. Broadway, #224, Chicago, IL 60613

A rock & roll zine by and for grrrls. Interviews with bands like Tribe 8, 7 Year Bitch, Velocity Girl. Book reviews, comix, and articles/rants about being alive and female.

Utandande

$10/year (4 issues) from: Utandande, 1711 E. Spruce St., Seattle, WA 98122-5728; 206-323-6592; fax 206-329-9355

For fans of Zimbabwean marimba and *mbira* music. Also for fans of traditional music and percussion in general. Performance info, workshops, and resource guides.

The Wire

$50/year (11 issues) from: Yellowstone, Int'l, 87 Burlews Court, Hackensack, NJ 07601; in Europe: The Wire, 45-46 Poland St., London W1V 3DF, England; fax 071-287-4767

Classy jazz, world and progressive music zine from England. Interviews with current stars, profiles of influential past and up-and-coming stars, info on small label releases, and personal musical essays by authors such as Greil Marcus. Plus reviews.

Crammed Mail Order catalog free from: Crammed Mail Order, 341 Lafayette St., #167, NY, NY 10012

Experimental, soundtrack, progressive and world music recordings: John Lurie, Fred Frith, Peter Principle, Hector Zazou, Tuxedomoon, etc.

Firebird catalog free from: Firebird Distributing, P.O. Box 1636, Pacifica, CA 94044

Distributor of imported recordings in the U.S.; electronic, progressive rock, zouk, rai, etc., from France, Spain, Canada, the Caribbean, Morocco, Algeria, etc.

Green Linnet catalog free from: Green Linnet Records, 43 Beaver Brook Rd., Danbury, CT 06810; 800-468-6644; fax 203-730-0345

Celtic and original North American folk, with a little bluegrass. **Xenophile**, a sub-label, specializes in worldbeat.

Insomnia Records catalog free from: Insomnia Records, P.O. Box 86308, LA, CA 90086

Distributes a multitude of indy labels: Restless, ROIR, Triple X, Taang!, Touch and Go, Knitting Factory Works, Cargo, Estrus, Alternative Tentacles, etc.

Japan Overseas catalog $5 (1 year/6 catalogs) from: Japan Overseas, 6-1-21 Ueshio, Tennoji-ku, Osaka 543, Japan; 06-771-8573; fax 06-771-8583

Japanese indy music, experimental, rock, industrial. Also zines and comix.

Lovely Music catalog free from: Lovely Music, 10 Beach St., NY, NY 10013

Twentieth-century experimental, New Music and progressive jazz recordings. Also, videos and books.

Playing by Ear catalog free from: Playing By Ear, P.O. Box 36057, Baltimore, MD 21286

Industrial, ambient, noise. An excellent collection of discs.

RAS catalog free from: RAS Records, P.O. Box 42517, Washington, D.C. 20015; 301-588-9641; fax 301-588-7108

Reggae specialists for 10 years. Lots of styles here: vocals, dub, DJ style, ska, rock steady. They also carry worldbeat titles, videos and books.

Reference Recordings catalog free from: Reference Recordings, P.O. Box 77225X, San Francisco, CA 94107; 415-355-1892; fax 415-355-1949

Audiophile recordings of modern jazz and popular classical pieces.

Roots & Rhythm catalog free from: Roots & Rhythm, 6921 Stockton Ave., El Cerrito, CA 94530; 510-525-1494; fax 510-525-2904

Distributors of folk, blues, vintage jazz and rock, world music, country, bluegrass. Also related books and zines.

Smithsonian/Folkways Mail Order, 416 Hungerford Dr., #320, Rockville, MD 20850; 301-443-2314; fax 301-443-1819

Archival recordings of music, celebrations and rituals from around the world.

T.E.Q. Music? catalog for SAE and 1 IRC from: T.E.Q. Music?, P.O. Box 87, Ilford, Essex IG1 3HJ, England; voice/fax 44-081-51803092

Creators of MFTEQ (Music from the Empty Quarter) CD/book series. Number 1 is a 124-page book and CD with 16 tracks from industrial, noise and ambient bands: Attrition, Black Tape For A Blue Girl, Controlled Bleeding, Chris & Cosey, Blackhouse, etc.

Uncommon Music catalog free from: Uncommon Music, P.O. Box 3589, Saxonville, MA 01701-0605; 508-820-4440; fax 508-820-7769

Modern classical, jazz, folk, and country, mostly from artists in the northeast of the U.S.

Utandande Gifts catalog free from: Utandande, 1711 E. Spruce St., Seattle, WA 98122-5728; 206-323-6592; fax 206-329-9355

Music and books for fans of Shona marimba and *mbira* music.

We Never Sleep catalog free from: We Never Sleep, P.O. Box 92, Denver, CO 80201; fax 303-778-6805

Avant-garde, punk, experimental, *edgey* music, videos, and books. Extremely high-quality selection of artists.

Whirled Discs catalog free from: Whirled Discs, P.O. Box 151290, San Rafael, CA 94915-1290; voice/fax 415-454-4420

World music from Africa, Latin America, India, the Caribbean. Interesting and informative descriptions of the music and artists in their catalog.

Fig. 166.
SYSTÈME NERVEUX DE L'HOMME.

Nerfs
du bras

Nerfs de
la jambe

THE NET

Introduction—The Net

Russia had the Bomb. Cuba almost had the Bomb. Communist China was on its way to getting the Bomb. The early '60s weren't what you'd call a stable time in world politics. "The Powers That Be" in the U.S., on the off chance that someone was going to lob a multi-megaton warhead our way, decided that they needed a way to communicate and to run command-and-control operations outside of normal channels. They handed the problem over to the Cold War idea boys at the Rand Corporation, and announced their daring proposal to the world in 1964. The communication problem could be overcome with a simple (and from a '90s perspective, obvious) system—a network with no central authority, and one that would work even when huge chunks of it were removed.

If you think this last bit sounds like a basic description of the Internet, you're right. The system we now use daily to send each other email mash notes and Star Trek trivia quizzes is an expanded version of the old military system, known as ARPANET. The name Internet came into play much later, and only after a lot of non-military networks hooked themselves to each other through ARPANET. Even when the military was still using the system, civilians couldn't get into their files (well, in theory), but both techie nerds and Minuteman-launching generals could use the same computer system at the same time. Eventually, the military boys built their own system, called MILNET, based on the original ARPANET principles. By the time they went away, however, the Internet was up and running, connecting scientists, hackers, college students, pranksters, weird artists, and visionaries from all over the world.

Of course, being an old military system, the Internet (or simply "Net") had never been exactly easy to navigate. You had to learn a whole new set of complex commands to move around, and if you screwed up, you'd probably get boinked out of the system, and have to start all over again. Still, the thing worked. Now the Internet is connected through thousands of "nodes." A node is any computer that's an official part of the Net system. A node can be a university, office, museum, important individual or computer bulletin board or conferencing system. Many BBS and conferencing systems exist simply as front-ends to the Net, making it easier to get into the Net and move around. There are regional systems all over the U.S. (and in most of the rest of the world). If you don't know of any systems in your area, check the newsstands for local computer zines, or call the computer department of a local college or university. You can also use some of the publications (such as *Boardwatch* and *3W*) reviewed in this chapter to get started. And after you read, "A Young Person's Guide to the Internet," by Steve Lombardi and Phil Rzewski, you'll be ready for some heavy netsurfing.

For readers who are already on the Net, this chapter also has a listing of some interesting FTP sites (where you can download text and graphics for free) and WWW homepages (the World Wide Web is an interface that lets you access text, pictures and sound through your home computer; you need a special computer account and software to use the WWW). And for anyone who wants amusing and bizarre missives in their online mail box, we have some email lists you can join.

EFF's Guide to the Internet

free via anonymous FTP: ftp.eff.org/pub/Net_info/EFF_Net_Guide

Formerly **The Big Dummy's Guide to the Internet**, this excellent guide for novices was put together by the Electronic Frontier Foundation, an information and lobbying group dedicated to keeping the net as open and free as possible. MIT Press is publishing a book version of EFF's guide, called **Everybody's Guide to the Internet.** If you know how to ftp, however, you can get the same information for free from EFF's archives. For more information about EFF, write to: The Electronic Frontier Foundation, 1001 G Street NW, Suite 950 E, Washington DC 20001; 202-347-5400; fax 202-393-5509; BBS: 202-638-6120; email: ask@eff.org.

The Internet Directory

by Eric Braun
$25; Fawcett Columbine
1994; 704 pp.

A sort of phone book for the Net. **The Internet Directory** is 700 pages of downloading, accessing, emailing, and telneting info for Usenet newsgroups, online library catalogs, FTP and gopher sites, WAIS resources, WWW clients, electronic journals and text sources, mailing lists and more. **The Internet Directory** is a no-frills publication—just pages and pages of addresses and site info, but if information is what you want, this is the book to get.

Internet Starter Kit

by Adam C. Engst
$29.95; Hayden Books
1993; 641 pp.

Quite a package. Not only do you get a telephone directory-size book on navigating the Net, but you also get a free disk that comes with all the basic software you need to get going! Included on the Macintosh disk are Eudora 1.4, Fetch 2.1.1, InterSLIP 1.01, MAC TCP 2.0.2, StuffIt Expander 3.07, and TurboGopher 1.07. If you don't know what the hell the names on that list mean, don't sweat it. The book comes with simple explanations of, for instance, gopher sites and why you might want to use them. This isn't a book about lofty communications theories, but about getting into the Net and to work, as quickly and easily as possible. Currently, there are Macintosh and PC versions of the **Internet Starter Kit.**

Net Guide

by Peter Rutten, Albert F. Bayers III and Kelly Maloni
1994; 384 pp.
$22 ppd from: Michael Wolff & Co., 1633 Broadway, 27th Floor, NY, NY 10019; 212-841-1572; fax 212-841-1539; email: mwolff@ypn.com

The Internet without tears. This is the most user-friendly online guide around, a highly illustrated *TV Guide*-ish listing of where and how to find what you want on the Net by topic (books, jazz, China, Business News, baseball, AIDS, cyberpunk, sex, the environment, history, etc.). For info on online updates, email: mwolff@ypn.com.

The Whole Internet

by Ed Krol
$24.95; O'Reilly & Associates; 1992; 376 pp.
An excellent basic guide to finding your way around the Net, and making use of the tools you find there (FTP, archie, gopher, WWW, etc.). It also has appendices with a glossary of Net terms, international email codes and descriptions of connection services.

Boardwatch

$36/year (12 issues; $99 overseas) from: Boardwatch, 8500 W. Bowles Ave., #210, Littleton, CO 80123; 800-933-6038; fax 303-973-3731; email: jack.rickard@boardwatch.com

A glossy monthly zine that covers the worlds of computer bulletin boards (BBSs) and computer-telecommunications. Each issue has articles on new BBSs, modems, and communications software, as well as primers on how to use arcane Net tools. There's also news from the big BBSs and directories of local area BBSs (the April/May issue featured Baltimore boards).

3W

$45/year (6 issues; £24 UK & Europe; £30 foreign) from: 3W Magazine, 461 W. 49th St., #338, NY, NY 10019; 212-388-2830; fax 212-399-0577; email: subs@ukartnet.demon.co.uk

"The Internet with a human face." This zine out of London tracks doings on the Net from a global perspective. There's a bit of everything you could want—news, gossip, product and book reviews, Internet access for Europe and North America. When you want to see the evolution of cyberspace as it happens, *3W* is the place to go.

A Young Person's Guide to the Internet

Cyberspatial Consciousness and Computer Literacy in One Easy to Swallow Capsule.

By Steve Lombardi and Phil Rzewski

The Internet is big and getting bigger. According to *Boardwatch* magazine, it doubled in size between 1991 and 1992—both in the number of networks that comprise it and the amount of data passing through its infrastructure. And it's still growing.

What it is, what is out there on it, how you can access it, and the benefits of doing so are the topics of this article. Those with a deep hatred of computers, either due to bad personal experience or simple unfamiliarity, are probably about to turn the page to find the comix section or something. Don't. Hang in there. We'll cover the basics quickly and get to the fun stuff. You'll find that the Internet has something of interest for everyone and you'll thank us for making you stay.

WHAT IT IS

The Internet is about the closest thing we have today to "cyberspace," a term coined by William Gibson in his 1984 novel **Neuromancer** to describe the superset of all electronic data and society's interaction with it. This network of the future is a multisensorial experience somewhere between hallucination and out-of-body phenomena that allows a user to meld with the matrix, visualizing data constructs as if he or she was "there." The Internet, however, has a less exciting interface: generally a spew of text and simple graphics with a COMMAND-LINE PROMPT for your keyboard input—no need to jack in through a black market Ono-Sendai or achieve oneness with your machine to access the wonders of the Net—but if you're a geek purist you may consider a brain-implanted RS-232 straight to your noggin.

So here's telecommunications in a nutshell: A "modem" hooked to your home computer allows you to call other computers across town or around the world by translating the computer's data into a high-pitched squeal that is then sent over a phone line and retranslated back into data by another computer. Once connected to this other computer—the "host" machine—you can upload and download data such as software, graphic images, or even something as complex as a musical composition you've created. You can send electronic mail to other users of the host system and receive the same, or you can post public messages to discussion groups (or "conferences"), thus participating in round-table discussions on a variety of topics.

Small personal computer bulletin board systems that offer these features ("BBSs," as they are known) are everywhere—typically, a few exist in any given area code. Local BBSs tend to take on a flavor the way local bars and clubs do. You've got jock bars, queer bars, dance clubs, etc....For variety you go bar-hopping or perhaps you prefer to find a favorite and stick. It's much the same with BBSs: they seem to cater to people's tastes. Geek boards, game boards, 1-900-style personals, pirate boards...you get the idea. Many find themselves wanting to communicate with more people from a wider geographic sampling, which is where large-scale networks come in, with the Internet—really a telecommunications supernet comprised of smaller regional networks accessible from one jumping-off point—being the granddaddy of them all. Many of these local BBSs also offer access to the Internet for a reasonable fee.

So you've got a cheap personal computer, a modem, some telecommunications software, and an Internet account (more on actually acquiring all this later). What next? Well, just about anything.

WHAT'S OUT THERE

Usenet

Usenet is the component of the Internet that features BBS-style message bases. These "newsgroups" are areas where you can post articles on a specific subject and read what others have contributed. Currently there are many hundreds of newsgroups to choose from, ranging in subject matter from current events to tasteless humor, sports, bestiality, space exploration, cooking... and more newsgroups are added on a daily basis. A Japanese noise band touring through your town and you're not sure if you want to shell out the eight bucks? Check out Usenet's alternative/industrial newsgroup (rec.music.industrial as it is called in Usenet's somewhat enigmatic nomenclature) as odds are pretty good that someone has posted a review of an earlier show. My new favorite is the folklore group (alt.folklore.urban), where folks with a lot of time on their hands prove or disprove nutty high school rumors and stuff your grandpa once told ya. (I'll bet you didn't know that not a single case of a kid getting Halloween treats stuffed with razors has ever been officially reported to the cops.)

An active group like alt.cyberpunk can have a hundred or more articles posted per day, so be prepared to flush many hours down the toilet wading through "noise" for the good stuff, even if you find only a few groups of interest. And unless you're a total blockhead with no interest in anything but your own death, you will. Not to say there's anything wrong with a preoccupation with your own death; in fact, there's a Usenet group devoted to the topic (rec.holiday.suicide).

Email

Email is a personal means of communication between a small number of folks. Every user of the Internet has a unique address where private mail can be sent (mine, for example, is stlombo@acm.rpi.edu). Email can be a simple text message or—properly translated into ASCII and later retranslated back into binary code—even contain an audio sample or graphic image. I can send a message to one friend or a predefined mailing list instantly. The message will be held in the recipient's "mailbox" until s/he dials in to retrieve it. This privacy eliminates the aforementioned noise, but it shares with Usenet another major communication hurdle: its asynchronous nature. Email is fast but response is rarely instantaneous. Computer-mediated conferencing systems ("CMCs") address this problem nicely. Here's Doogie with a timely overview.

CMCs

One of the ways many people get started in the Net is through a computer-mediated conferencing system, a way to talk to several other people who could be anywhere else in the world. It's like being on one of those silly 1-900 chat lines, but it's cheap (usually free) and the conversation can have real quality.

Here is a copy of a conversation I had on a local system called "Clover." Keep in mind that what you see is exactly what was on my computer screen. It includes things I typed and things people typed back as well as esoteric CMC terminology. To "say something" to the discussion I simply type "-def;" (shorthand for "I wanna send to the default discussion") and then type what I want to say. The computer tells me when the message is sent to everyone else and a few seconds later someone will see it and may write something in return. The cycle continues. Here is an excerpt:

> -def; g'day everyone. i'm writing a small article on net stuff for a local zine and they are interested in a log of a clover-like chat. so if anyone would like to help out and

say something interesting, shocking, or obscene go right ahead.(message sent to - default.)

- From Prisoner [class plan] [Then Follow], to - default:

- "interesting, shocking, or obscene"?...

-def; ok, ok... so it was a bit redundant.(message sent to - default.)

-def; i feel like i just walked up to a comedian and said "say something funny."(message sent to -default.)

- From Prisoner [class plan] [Then Follow], to - default:

- what kind of zine is this?...

-def; what kind? small... underground... "Reign of Toads."(message sent to - default.)

- From clueless [—To the Union!], to -default: -Reign of Toads? Interesting title.. is it a local thing?

-def; local indeed. the guy who does it lives in albany.(message sent to -default.)

You ever try and take a home movie and then have all the people act like they had nothing to say? At any rate, this at least allows you to see what it looks like. This could have gone on for as long as there were people to talk to—and there always are. You can usually find something to debate on (politics, gay rights, or computer-related topics are usually things you can get people going on at any time). Also, if you have something you need help with, be it computerish or "How do I get mustard stains off the couch?," there's bound to be someone around who will know. The advantage of a CMC over something like Usenet is that the people are there and can assist or entertain you in a matter of seconds.

CMCs have many fun-related features as well. "Connect," another relatively famous CMC on the east coast, used to have a facility to allow users to play Uno while online. Internet Relay Chat—or "IRC," a global conferencing system covering everything from new computer hardware to Ren and Stimpy rehash sessions—has a facility to allow the transfer of files through the system. This way if I was talking to someone who had a great new game for his computer, he could send it to my machine in just a few seconds without having to leave the conference.

File Transfer Protocol

The Internet, remember, is made up of a vast network of computing machines primarily owned and operated by quasi-fascist organizations like NASA, the U.S. Army, General Electric, your local university, etc....Many of these sites have, out of the kindness of their hearts, set aside some of their disk resources for use by you and me. This means I can enter a command to connect me instantly to wherever I need to be and retrieve files from said location. For example, entering the following at my terminal...

ftp wuarchive.wustl.edu

...would hook me up with the massive data archive at Washington University. When prompted to log on, it is customary to enter one's email address, but the username "anonymous" requires no specific password. Now I'm connected and can search the directories for public domain software, bitmapped graphics, video games, electronic zines, whatever...downloading what I need to my machine at an alarming rate—usually better than 10K per second. An archive of this size often contains hundreds of MEGS of files.

Archie

Now with the bevy of fascist organizations that we know exist, combined with the fact that many of them devote gigabytes of storage to these FTP archives, you might think it would be next to impossible to efficiently find a particular file. The archie server was developed to eliminate this dilemma.

Imagine for a moment being called Jughead from a young age. Archie is every FTP geek's best friend. Each night while you and I sleep, archie logs in to anonymous FTP sites all over creation. Each site gets hit monthly or so. I think there's currently about a thousand of them containing like...like...like a terabyte worth of data, man—more by the time you read this. Whatever file names exist at any location are deposited into this big database to await your queries. Archie will then tell you where to FTP to find your file. To use archie you need to telnet to connect to an archie server. Telnet is merely a protocol for connecting two machines:

telnet archie.ans.net

In a moment you'd get a LOGIN prompt. Just enter "archie." Let's say you wanted to find a file called pigsex.lzh (many do, more on that later). You would enter:

prog pigsex.lzh

Soon after, archie would list all of the FTP sites—if any—containing your file. You don't necessarily need to know the whole filename either: archie has powerful search capabilities, featuring pattern matching, etc.... With a bit of practice any file can be found anywhere in about 60 seconds (off-peak). Then one simply FTPs to the address archie provides to retrieve the file.

FTP works both ways. You can upload data as well as download it, making these sites an efficient and powerful way to exchange information. As a special interest group arises (like zine publishers or student activists, say) with a requirement for storing data (like text files and contact lists) in an accessible place, someone with Internet access and system privileges may very well start an FTP site. In recent times the system administrators of many of these sites have tried to control (i.e., censor) what files are stored on their systems for worldwide distribution. But, as Doogie explains, the task of stopping geeks from distributing forbidden files is difficult at best.

Pig Sex

There was an era in anonymous FTP where you could find anything if you were willing to look hard enough. In very obvious places I found things like *Phrack* magazine (an "ezine" which taught how to hack, build explosives, and break the law in other interesting ways), pirated software...and tons of pornographic pictures.

Pornography had to be about the biggest thing on the Net for a long time. It seemed like every college, business, government and privately-owned machine had a library of pornographic pictures, be it small or large. These pictures are electronically scanned from magazines and other sources into image files that almost any computer can be used to view. The most common of these formats are GIF (a Graphics Interchange Format developed by the whitebread pay-computer network CompuServe) and JPEG. Basically, if I bought the newest issue of *Nuns & Nazis* magazine and scanned a picture from it into a GIF, all you'd need is a program on your computer that could display GIF picture files on the screen. I send you the picture (through FTP or email) and then you could look at it.

The Net was flooded with GIFs. Eventually picture files became such a load on the Internet that the people paying the bills began to take notice. The group that whined the most was the National Science Foundation. They said that the only things you could store through anonymous FTP had to have some "educational" value. If a site continued to offer pornography, the NSF would simply shut off the site's network access. They would then have no mail, no Usenet, no legitimate FTP, nothing. All the pictures disappeared.

Strangely enough, though, a group was soon formed under Usenet to distribute the pictures. People would "uuencode" them (a UNIX command) in a text format that could be posted to the Usenet group for all to see. The idea behind this strategy is that a company getting Usenet news can easily say "I don't want this group" and it won't be sent to their site. Alt.binaries.pictures.erotica has been up and running for a few years now with no big complaints.

But getting things off Usenet, to be honest, is a royal pain in the ass when compared with transferring over FTP. A few people have set up "hidden" FTP sites in places where the NSF wouldn't think to look. They then tell their friends about it and say "Don't tell anyone!" The site tends to last for a few weeks or months, until someone tells a stupid person who posts a message on Usenet saying "Hey! If you want porno pictures they're available by FTPing to host blah.blah.blah!" The last time this happened—and I am completely serious here—in the first 24 hours after the post was made 18,000 people tried to FTP to that site. Needless to say, long before the NSF even began to care, the site had to cut off its own Net connection to keep people from slowing it down so much by logging on and searching for porn.

MUDs

Aside from CMCs and pornography, there are more traditional forms of recreation available through the Net. People have taken the time to write programs which give the feeling of playing a real game with other people when, in fact, they might be halfway across the earth. Some games which are well-supported on the Net are Chess, Bridge, and Go.

Another type of game is a Multi-User Dungeon, or "MUD." These systems have people connecting and talking to each other from all over the world, much like a CMC, but in a MUD you are actually a character in a computerized role-playing environment. Your virtual world contains all the features of a real one—other people, cities, roads, mountains, forests, money, and of course animals—but also things you wouldn't find a lot in the real world, like monsters, magic, treasure, and weapons.

The purpose of most MUDs, like many role-playing games, is to gain "experience" by slaying monsters or solving puzzles. On the MUDs I was most familiar with, as you gained experience you became more powerful and harder to kill. When you had enough experience you became a "wizard" and were given a part of the virtual world to call your own. Wizards would then "add" to the world by programming their own monsters and puzzles. This allowed the MUD to become larger and different every week.

What I have described is only a certain type of MUD. I've heard people talk about several other types, many of which sound even more like real life. One woman I spoke to was preparing for a MUD wedding where characters, not people, were getting married. She was "baking a cake": in other words, she was writing a program to "make cake." Boggled MY mind.

Some other guys I knew were trying to write a program to "grow flowers." When you used the program to "plant seeds," the flowers would grow day by day as you played the MUD. If you were a character walking through a room where flowers were growing, the computer would tell you "There are some flowers starting to sprout over to the left." And, sometime later, "There are some flowers in full bloom in a pot near the door." There are so many different MUDs that there's no way I could describe them all.

It's important to mention how utterly addicting MUDs can be. When I got heavily involved with them I used to MUD from about 10 p.m. to 6 a.m. every night. Fortunately I was just a young high school lad on my summer vacation and I outgrew it soon enough, but I know people who take it so seriously that they divide their lives rather evenly among the two worlds: If they're awake 16 hours a day they'll spend eight hours in their real lives and eight hours MUDding— every day, all the time.

WWW

One very promising service that the Internet offers is the World Wide Web. The founders of the Web, CERN (European Particle Physics Laboratory), envisioned a world where all academic information would be freely available to anyone with an interest. As with all other aspects of the Net, the scope of the project has grown well beyond the walls of academe. There are Web servers providing song lyrics, on-line zines, car repair manuals, research libraries—whatever. CERN devised a system of browsers and servers—the Web browser being a program that you run on your local machine providing the user interface to the Web and communication with the server—a bank of links to documents and other multimedia objects (music, graphics, video...) located around the world.

Information access through the Web is designed to be random access. You may be reading the script of a play and actually jump to a review of a live performance. These two documents may be on servers 1000 miles apart—it makes no difference. Access is transparent and you the reader never see the ugly nuts and bolts that glue all of this together. This non-linear means of access, commonly known as hypertext or hypermedia, is becoming more and more common on the Net. AT&T and MCI can only prophesy the future in their respective Net-wise 30 second spots as they scramble madly to get a foot in a wide-open door they've ignored for years.

For more info on WWW send email to timbl@info.cern.ch. Better yet, to try out the Web, telnet to info.cern.ch. You will be greeted by a simple command line browser.

WHO RUNS IT?

It's been said that no single entity possesses the power to shut down the Internet. Believe it. Even organizations with a lot of control over the Net such as the National Science Foundation could only cripple it by shutting down the section they maintain. It's just too sprawled. Maybe that leads to why certain organizations (three guesses) are vying to control these massive nets—aka, Al Gore's "national data highway." Nice analogy, Al. Highways: potholes to inconvenience you, toll booths to restrict access and keep accounts fat, cops patrolling to nab rule-breakers.

Once again the Japanese can look at us and laugh. They have already committed to having fiber optic lines run into every home within 12 years. Bandwidth to carry realtime digital video right to your doorstep. Congressman Frederick Boucher refers to this as "deployment over the last mile." Face it: running a mammoth backbone is really no amazing feat. Getting access from the bone to the home is. In this country, Joe Citizen will probably never see the wonders of 56K+ transmissions to his home in his lifetime.

HOW YOU CAN ACCESS IT

Now hopefully a lot of you are wondering how to get access to the Internet. First the easy part. As mentioned above, you'll need a home computer, a modem, and some communications software. If you don't already own one, a cheap used PC clone can be had for as little as $300 (watch the local classifieds), and your basic 2400 baud modem might be $50. Software is cheap, too: plenty of basic computer systems come bundled with telecom programs or you can pick up a shareware product like Procomm or Telix for peanuts from a software distributor or a fellow computer geek and pay for it when you decide you like it (around $30). There are entire books devoted to the topic of shopping for a used or cheap computer and monthly tomes like *Computer Shopper* (available at damn near any newsstand) offer no-name "bargains" galore. Caveat emptor. Now the tough part: an account.

If you're a student, check with the computer department at your school. You may be entitled to an account or you may already have one and not know it. Many mid- to large-sized businesses also have access. Ask around the lunchroom. Local BBSs may offer Internet gateways. You'll have to check the boards in your area. As a last (and, for most, only) resort, there are a host of commercial services available. They charge an hourly or monthly fee for Internet access. Two of the best deals I know of are a connection via Portal (voice phone 408-973-9111) or Delphi. The latter even offers 5 free hours of Internet access for new users. With your modem dial 1-800-365-4636 to try them out. Pick up the latest *Boardwatch* and scan the ads for others.

DISCLAIMER

This has been a rather bombastic look at the Internet. It may seem overwhelming, but it really isn't. Score an account and try the services one at a time. A number of Usenet groups exist to discuss the Internet itself, connections, means of access, etc. The Full text of Al Gore's "highway" bill as well as info on other national Net initiatives can be had by FTPing to nis.nsf.net and looking in the nsfnet directory. I can be reached at stlombo@acm.rpi.edu and Doogie is right next door at kutcha@acm.rpi.edu.

BBS List

wuarchive.wustl.edu: mirrors/msdos/bbslists/
BBSs of all types and in all regions are listed here.

Cypherpunk

soda.berkeley.edu: /pub/cypherpunks
An archive of info by and for encryption and privacy mavens. PGP and other encryption tools, blind servers info, digital. cash, political action.

Electronic Frontier Foundation

ftp.eff.org
EFF is a combo information dispenser, lobbying group, legal defense organizer and gadfly group for the Net. Its goal is to keep the Net as open and free as possible. Their FTP site has a wealth of Net-related documents: zines, academic papers, timely alerts for the Net community, Computer Academic Freedom Archives, and Internet guides such as EFF's Guide to the Internet (formerly, **The Big Dummy's Guide to the Internet**). Logon and look around.

Extropianism

lynx.cs.wisc.edu: /pub/ExI-Essay
"For sharing libertarian, free-market, life-extensionist and other Extropian ideas with bright, like-minded individuals around the globe."

FTP Sites List

pilot.njin.net: pub/ftp-list/ftp.list

Government Stuff

wiretap.spies.com
This site contains many U.S. government-related documents, including the texts of many of Clinton's speeches, FOIA (Freedom of Information Act) info, texts of constitutions from around the world, historical documents, etc.

The Hacker Crackdown

Europe: ftp.germany.eu.net:
pub/books/sterling/crackdown
North America: ftp.eff.org:
pub/Publications/Bruce_Sterling/Hacker_
Crackdown
Bruce Sterling's non-fiction book about law and order on the information frontier is available online on the above sites:

Internet Basics

nnsc.nsf.net: nsfnet/internet-basics.eric-digest

Internet maps (Europe)

eunet.fi: nic/pub/netinfo/maps/

LERI

bertha.pyramid.com: pub
The archives of the Leri (Tim Leary) mailing list. Metaprogramming, philosophy, evolution, drugs, personal freedom.

New User's Questions

nic.merit.edu: documents/fyi/FYI_04.TXT

The Occult

Some interesting occult material can be found on slopoke.mlb.semi.harris.com via anonymous ftp. This site holds complete ASCII versions of books by Aleister Crowley, the Church of Set, books on Enochian Magick, Old Slack, and more. Check out all the directories in /pub/.—Joseph Matheny

Project Gutenberg

mrcnext.cso.uiuc.edu:/pub/etext
Online book access has been a dream ever since people realized you could do more with computers than crunch really, really big numbers really, really fast. These online texts will never replace the real books, but

they will give everyone with a modem access to the words themselves. This will be a benefit to students, researchers, and anyone who doesn't happen to live near the Library of Congress. This site contains the current text holdings, everything from **Tarzan** to **Ivanhoe** to **Frankenstein** to **A Connecticut Yankee in King Arthur's Court.**

Radical Literature

To see what may be the largest online library of radical literature cruise over to etext.archive.umich.edu. There you can download (for free!) complete works ranging from **Moby Dick** to Hakim Bey's **T.A.Z.** The site also houses files on a myriad of topics—radical politics, fascist and reactionary literature, fiction, poetry, cyberpunk magazines, mailing list archives and zines of all kinds. It is accessible by anonymous FTP and gopher protocols.—Joseph Matheny

Survival Research Laboratories

ftp.srl.org

Mark Pauline's robot performance group has their own FTP site. Like their shows, it's a noisy, chaotic, and ever-changing terrain. Generally, it's only online from 12 p.m. to 6 a.m., but try logging in at other times. You might get lucky. The site has lots of graphic files from SRL shows in GIF and JPEG formats. There is data on upcoming shows, and info on ordering SRL videos, posters, etc. Users are encouraged to upload any scurrilous and vile material that might entertain or edify other users. Also, anyone with access to high-level, sensitive or classified technical information should feel free to stop by and upload all you want. SRL is always in the market for technical data.

WAX or the Discovery of Television Among the Bees

ftp.rahul.net:/pub/atman/UTLCD-preview/assorted-images/

Still images from David Blair's brilliant "electronic movie" are available online—with Blair's permission. The files are called "tveye.jpg" and "wxfigurs.jpg"

Windows Software

ftp.cica.indiana.edu:/pub/pc/win3

A large archive of Windows software and related information.

To make full use of the text, graphics and sound capabilities of the World Wide Web (WWW), you need several pieces of software, all of which can be found free via anonymous FTP. The basic software you need is called Mosaic. There are versions available for Macs and Windows at the site: ftp.ncsa.uiuc.edu. For Windows, look in the directory, "PC/Mosaic;" for Macs, look in "Mac/Mosaic."

To use Mosaic, you must be running SLIP, PPP or other TCP/IP networking on your computer. You can arrange SLIP and PPP accounts through local Internet providers. Check your local BBSs for suggestions. If you can't get a SLIP or PPP access, you can still use Lynx, a text-only system, available on many BBSs.

The Quadralay Corporation of Austin, Texas, has developed the first commercially-supported WWW browser. The basic package is called GWHIS Viewer, and it can operate as a compete front end to the Net, supporting WWW, gopher, FTP, telneting, Net News, and email. Reportedly, GWHIS Viewer will also support public key encrypted digital signatures. The basic package is $249 retail. For more information: Quadralay Corporation, 8920 Business Park Dr., Austin, Texas 78759; 512-346-9199; fax 512-346-8990; email: info@quadralay.com; WWW Server: www.quadralay.com.

WWW Home Pages

alt.cyberpunk FAQ
http://bush.cs.tamu.edu/ pub/misc/erich/alt.cp.faq.html

Analogue Heaven (music)
http://www.cs.washington.edu/homes/map/analog/analog.html

ANIMA (Arts Network for Integrated Media Applications)
http://wimsey.com/anima/ANIMAhome.html

BDSM (Bondage/Submission Sadism/Masochism)
http://elbow.cs.brown.edu:8100/dcr/bdsm/bdsm.html

Bridge Playing
http://www.cs.vu.nl/users/staff/sater/bridge/bridge-on-the web.html

Charles Stross' science fiction stories
http://tardis.ed.ac.uk/~charlie/fictionhome.html

Commonplace Book on Writers and Writing
http://sunsite.unc.edu/ibic/Writing-CPB.html

Cryptography Export Issues
http://www.cygnus.com/~gnu/export.html

F5 (Factsheet 5, the Zine of Zines)
http://kzsu.stanford.edu/uwi.html

FAQs (Frequently Asked Questions archives)
http://www.cis.ohio-state.edu/hypertext/faq/usenet/FAQ-List.html

FBI home page
http://naic.nasa.gov/fbi/FBI_homepage.html

Fringeware
http://io.com/commercial/fringeware/home.html

Gateway to Darkness (music)
http://coe1.engr.umbc.edu/~vijay2/home.html

General Music Information
http://www.cs.cmu.edu:8001/afs/cs.cmu.edu/user/jdg/www/music.html

Hong Kong Cinema
http://www.mdstud.chalmers.se/hkmovie/

IUMA (Internet Underground Music Archive)
http://sunsite.unc.edu/ianc/IUMA/index.html

Libertarian Party
http://www.lp.org/lp/lp.html

New Russia-American Friends and Partners
http://solar.rtd.utk.edu/friends/home.html

New World Headquarters (WWW zine)
http://www.wimsey.com/~jmax/index.html

Nexus elist
http://www.ifi.uio.no/~mariusw/nexus/

Nippon Telegraph and Telephone Corporation http://iikk.inter.net/tomi-gaya.html

Oceania (The Atlantis Project)
http://saturn.uaamath.alaska.edu/~kane/-oceania_start.html

O'Reilly & Associates Global Network News
http://nearnet.gnn.com/GNN-ORA.html

Republican Party Platform
http://neptune.corp.harris.com/platform.html

Rice Design Alliance's VIRTUAL CITY
http://riceinfo.rice.edu/ES/Architecture/RDA/VC/VirtualCity.html

Rob Ingram's Gothic Server (music)
http://web.cs.nott.ac.uk/~rji/index.html

Schwa (Alien Invasion Survival Products)
http://www.scs.unr.edu/homepage/rory/schwa/schwa.html

Science Television (educational TV company)
http://www.service.com/stv/

Singapore National Computer board
http://www.ncb.gov.sg

Stay-Free (independent music zine from North Carolina)
http://ruby.ils.edu/stayfree/home.htm

Supreme Court (Decisions from '93-94)
http://www.law.cornell.edu/lii.table.html

They Might Be Giants (the band)
http://ftp.netcom.com/pub/wubfur/TMBG/tmbg_home.html

Twin Peaks
http://pogo.wright.edu/TwinPeaks/TPHome.html

U2 (the band)
http://www-users.informatik.rwth-aachen.de/~kaldow/u2.html

Wired magazine
http://www.wired.com

Send an email request to any of these addresses to receive email, daily or weekly, covering a specific group a topic.

A Word A Day

request: wordsmith@viper.elp.cwru.edu
"I have created a wordserver which will mail out an English vocabulary word and its definition to the subscribers, every day."

David Koresh Documents

request:
dogface!podbox!wnations@cs.utexas.edu
Send a request to this address to receive an ASCII text version of David Koresh's "Seven Seals" document.—Joseph Matheny

Didjeridu List

request: listproc@varese.mills.edu
A list for people interested in the ancient Australian Aboriginal instrument, the did-jeridu (sic). In the message section, put on a line by itself: subscribe didjeridu first-name last-name.

FringeWare

request: fringeware-request@illumanati-.io.com
"An online marketplace for the fringes of technology, art and society. Weird software, strange gizmos, surreal expression, etc." Postings from an extremely interesting cross-section of Net-dwellers: wireheads, anarchists, cyber chix, science fiction writ-ers, journalists, etc.

Gender

request: owner-mail.gender@indiana.edu
Gender issues, and to get beyond trad-itional ideas of gender roles. In the Subject field enter "add me mail.gender".

Real Astrology

request: zenpride@well.sf.ca.us
Weekly astrology mailing list.

StickyFingers

request: sticky-request@cs.nott.ac.uk
For fans of the Stick, a musical instrument invented by Emmett Chapman. The Stick is a rectangular instrument with 10-12 strings (sort of an elongated guitar neck), that you play by tapping on the strings, piano-style.

Tibet

request: listserv@iubvm.ucs.indiana.edu
Questions and answers, news dispatches on Tibet, the Dalai Lama, the Tibetan people, Chinese and U.S. relations, etc.

XEPERA

request: xepera-l@astaroth.sacbbx.com
Serious discussions about the Temple of Set. "If you are considering joining the Temple of Set please read the Temple's General Information and Admissions Policies Letter." For email copy: jyouril@astaroth.sacbbx.com

Vampyres

request: listserv@guvm.ccf.georgetown.edu
Vampyre (sic) lore, facts, beliefs, books, movies, TV shows, filmographies, group stories, etc. Heavy traffic on this list. Be prepared for a lot of messages in your mail-box.

VIDEO

Introduction—Video

Video is one of those areas that just gets weirder and more interesting all the time. There are now so many little specialized distributors and producers that, with a little patience, persistence, and luck, there's probably a way to track down just about any video you might want. A book that will help start your search in Dennis Murry's **Offbeat Video Guide**, reviewed in this section.

One specialized area that was little more than a burgeoning cult when we did the first **Covert Culture Sourcebook** is Hong Kong video. Jackie Chan has always been a fringe favorite, but it's John Woo—whose directorial debut in Hollywood was the uneven *Hard Target*—that really made people sit up and bark. Woo combines the manic energy of traditional Hong Kong cinema with the balletic brutality of Peckinpah, the mythic gun-fighter of Sergio Leone and the street level spirituality of Martin Scorsese. It's because of directors like Woo and actors like Jackie Chan and Chow Yun Fat that HK cinema has become a very hot video item. To help you in your transformation into a real *gweilo* (literally "white devil"; it's Chinese street slang for honkies that hang around Chinatown, sort of the Chinese equivalent of "gringo."), we've put together a small list of must-see HK films. Of course, we've also listed places where you can get the films, and some publications to help you learn more about Hong Kong cinema.

In keeping with the Asian bent of the section, we have some Japanese animation titles to recommend. "Anime," as Japanese animation is more properly called, spans the spectrum from the somber and realistic style and subject matter of *Grave of the Fireflies* to the over-the-top sex and science fiction extravaganza, *Urotsukidoji: Legend of the Overfiend*.

We also take a look at some independent video titles, as well as video books, zines, and mail order sources.

The Killer

On its face, *The Killer* looks like a simple action-picture. But few relationships are simple in director John Woo's movies. The main themes he touches on in his films are friendship, loyalty, and betrayal. Danny Lee and Chow Yun Fat become unlikely allies in *The Killer*; unlikely, because Lee is a tough cop, while Fat is a smooth and accomplished hit man. They are drawn together by a cabaret singer (Sally Yip), whom Fat inadvertently blinded during a hit. Both Lee and Fat are suspicious of each other at first. In one amaz-

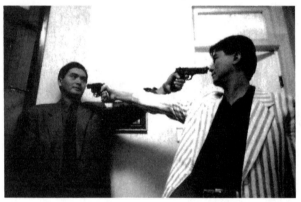

ing scene, they face off against each other in Yip's apartment, both with guns drawn and inches from the other's face; however, they keep their voices low and conversational, since neither wants to involve Yip. The scene is a masterful dance of tension, as is much of the film. When the violence comes, it's fast and brutal, combining both the visceral feel of Sam Peckinpah with the mythic quality of Sergio Leone. Woo is his own man, however, no mere impressionist.

The assassin (Chow Yun Fat) and the cop (Danny Lee) square off in John Woo's stylishly violent *The Killer*.

Within the violence, the relationships that have been built up over the film are still the most important element, and it's in that context that Woo convincingly portrays acts of personal sacrifice amid the intricately choreographed mayhem for which he's so famous. Other Woo films to look for are *Hard-Boiled, Bullet in Head, A Better Tomorrow 1* and *2*. With Chow Yun Fat, Danny Lee, Chu Kong, Tsang Kong, Sally Yip. Directed By John Woo. 1989.

One other note: Chow Yun Fat, the star of many of Woo's best films is an amazing talent. Not just a fine actor, but a true movie star, he has a presence that rivets you whenever he's on the screen. If any Asian actor is going to become a superstar in the West, the smart money will bet on Fat. Look for him in some of his other films, including *Full Contact, City War, God of Gamblers, Tiger on Beat, City on Fire,* and *Prison on Fire I and II.*

As Tears Go By

This brutal little gangster thriller about the underbelly of Hong Kong's underworld recalls nothing less than Martin Scorsese's *Mean*

Streets. The flip-side of John Woo's glamorous designer gangsters, *As Tears Go By* depicts gangland life as sordid, small-time and mean, driven by boredom and frustration. Back alley beatings and back door extortion is about as "glamorous" as it gets. Crossing a cool, high-tech style with savage realism, *Tears* is unequaled in its depiction of the adrenaline terrors of gangland life, and still manages to portray a potent, heartbreaking romance as well. Almost the entire cast won awards at Taiwan's "Oscars," the Golden Horse awards. First-time director Wong Kar-Wai brings a fierce energy and visual excitement to this violent, tragic tale. With Andy Lau, Maggie Cheung, Jackie Cheung, Alex Man. Directed by Wong Kar-Wai. 1988.—Tod Booth

Eastern Condors

This one belongs on any Best Action Movies of the '80s list, right alongside *Road Warrior* and *The Terminator.* Directed by and starring the portly but monumentally agile Samo Hung (to my mind, one of the great undiscovered action directors), *Eastern Condors* is, like many HK films, a variation on an American theme—in this case the good old Dirty Dozen-type suicide mission story. A group of hard-bitten, colorful criminals is sent into Vietnam to blow up an abandoned secret American missile cache before it—what else?—falls into enemy hands. The action starts the minute they parachute into

Actor/director Samo Hung squares off against an opponent in *Eastern Condors.* Both he and Jackie Chan honed their martial arts skills at the now-defunct Peking Opera school.

Vietnam and never lets up, as they team up with a trio of lethal female Cambodian guerrillas and fight their way through hostile territory to an amazing showdown with the best-bad-guy-in-the-business, Yuen Wah. *Eastern Condors* is a breathtaking, ferocious journey into the heart of darkness, an action epic as exciting as any you've ever seen. With Samo Hung, Yuen Biao, Haing S. Ngor, Joyce Godenzi, Yuen Wah. Directed by Samo Hung, 1986.—Tod Booth

Swordsman II

Producer-director team Tsui Hark and Ching Siu Tung (the *Chinese Ghost Story* series) may have produced their most exhilarating work yet. Set in mystical, long-ago China, it takes place one year after the events in *Swordsman* (you missed that one? Don't worry—this one's better anyway!). Martial arts superstar Jet Li stars as Swordsman Ling, who has decided to lay down his weapon and search for a retreat from the world of treachery and violence. But during his trek, he finds the evil Fong (Brigitte Lin) taking over the country. Fong has stolen the "Sacred Scroll" and, following its directions for improving his kung fu by changing his sex (!), has acquired tremendous magical powers. Mr./Ms. Fong also takes a liking to Ling, to complicate matters. And that's the least of the complications—there are enough plot twists to peel off another ten movies. The hallucinatory, ever-accelerating action takes *Swordsman II* into a new realm. The characters are just barely earthbound. They leap around like grasshoppers and, with a flick of the wrist, knock birds out of the sky or turn a man into mulch. Their swordfights are spectacular, high-velocity ballets. The film is, all at once, an elegant, hair-raising, hilarious, edge-of-your-seat experience. With Jet Li, Brigitte Lin, Michelle Li, Rosamund Kwan. Directed by Ching Siu Tung. 1992. —Tod Booth

Jackie Chan!

There's no way to present a Hong Kong movie list without a hefty kowtow to the King of Hong Kong cinema: Jackie Chan. He's possibly, and deservedly, the most popular movie personality in Asia—a director, writer, producer, choreographer as well as star (he's even a pop singer, too!). But above all, as a performer Chan is a miraculous synthesis of the history of the great physical movie stars, from Chaplin and Keaton to Douglas Fairbanks and Fred Astaire, from Jacques Tati to the Three Stooges. His films are unparalleled in their joyous physicality, their love of bodies in motion.—Tod Booth

Project A & Project A II

Simply put, Chan's masterworks, and two of the most lip-smackingly satisfying movies ever made. Chan plays Dragon Ma, an eager coast guard cop in turn-of-the-century HK, assigned to a district overrun with corrupt cops, mobsters, revolutionaries, mainland spies, and rapacious pirates. Together or separately, these films are a comic tour de force, electrifying blends of slapstick humor and staggering acrobatic action, where each dazzling set-piece tops the one before, culminating (in *Part II*) in an astonishing chase through Hong Kong's warehouse district. Chan's sparkling presence as a performer and deft touch as a director make the films as amiable as they are hair-raising. *Project A,* with Jackie Chan, Yuen Biao, Samo Hung. 1983. *Part II,* with Jackie Chan, Maggie Cheung, Carina Lau. 1987. Both directed by Jackie Chan. —Tod Booth

Minor-league coast guard cop, Jackie Chan makes a point in *Project A,* **in which he both starred and directed.**

Police Story

Jackie Chan plays a narcotics agent, a hot-dogging loner who, as a result of the mass destruction in the film's amazing opening scene, is demoted to protecting a key witness in a major drug trial. Chan loses his witness and ends up framed for murder, chased by both the cops and the bad guys. *Police Story's* climax takes place in one of Hong Kong's massive shopping malls—a rip-roaring display of Chan's martial arts wizardry and love of wanton havoc. With Jackie Chan, Brigitte Lin, Maggie Cheung. Directed by Jackie Chan. 1985.—Tod Booth

Chicken & Duck Talk

Hong Kong favorite Michael Hui produces, co-writes and stars in this rollicking comedy about warring restaurants. Hui runs a gloriously grungy BBQ duck joint where, though roaches are doing the backstroke in the soup and the staff spit-cleans the chopsticks, customers still line up for his fresh, lovingly hand-roasted ducks. He rules his world like a Chinese Jack Benny, brazenly exploiting his sad-sack staff (which includes his basset-faced real-life brother, Ricky) and too cheap to buy his devoted wife a birthday present. Suddenly, his little empire crumbles when, across the street, a new restaurant opens: Danny's Chicken Tornado, a sparkling, super-efficient American-style fast-food place. Danny lures away Hui's customers with slick TV commercials, free giveaways, and a crisply uniformed staff as polite and programmed as Moonies. *Chicken and Duck Talk* details Hui's efforts to catch up, using his own hilariously low-budget gimmicks. One of the movie's real pleasures is the down-to-earth way it presents Hong Kong's urban clutter and nutty intensity. It'll also make you rush down to Chinatown for the juiciest duck dinner you can find. With Michael Hui, Sylvia Chang, Ricky Hui. Directed by Clifton Ko.—Tod Booth

On The Run

Communist China takes over Hong Kong from its British owners in 1997. In *On The Run*, 1997 looms like the end of the world, and Hong Kong is a dark and terrifying city from which there is no way out. Hoping to escape is an honest cop, just trying to emigrate to Canada with his wife, until she is brutally murdered and he is framed for the crime. Hunted, confused and alone, his savior appears as a beautiful, icy hit-woman—the very one who gunned down his wife. Together, pursued by the police, they search the neon-lit city for the man who hired her, uncovering a trail of corruption that leads them deep into the heart of Hong Kong's fear of the future, and the desperate grab for cash to buy a way out. Brimming with astonishing twists and turns, and marked by standout performances by Yuen Biao and, especially, Pat Ha (as the coolest gun-for-hire you've ever seen), *On The Run* is one of the most hard-boiled and exciting *film noir* in years. With Yuen Biao, Pat Ha. Directed by Alfred Cheung. 1989.—Tod Booth

China's Last Eunuch

This is one of the strangest "bio-pics" you'll ever see. It tells the comic/tragic story of Lai Shi, whose big ambition as a little boy is to serve Emperor Pu Yi as a eunuch in the opulent Forbidden City. Dad lops off his "thing" (as the subtitles call it), stores it in a little sack (a eunuch must be buried with his penis or else be reincarnated as—horrors!—a woman), and sends the boy to meet the Emperor. Alas, shortly after he arrives at the Forbidden City, the Last Emperor is deposed. Lai Shi is cast out, along with the other castrati, forced to make his way in a world he was never prepared for. A surprisingly touching film, *China's Last Eunuch* strikes a fine balance between the absurd and the dramatic. It's also chock full of eunuch lore with which you can impress your friends at parties. Eliot Stein of the *Village Voice* picked *China's Last Eunuch* as one of his 1988 Ten Best. With Mok Siu Chung, Irene Wan, Samo Hung, Wu Ma. Directed by Jackie Cheung. 1988.—Tod Booth

Once Upon a Time in China

Whether he's producing or directing, Tsui Hark has a passion for epic-scale stories. While built around the romance of the legendary Chinese fighter, Wong Fey Hung (played by the charismatic Jet Li), *Once Upon a Time in China* is really the story of China itself, and its emergence into the 20th century. This was the first (and one of the best) of a whole wave of Chinese historical films. These period pieces have been both praised and criticized for their long looks backward. Some have accused them of being little more than a symptom of the uneasiness Hong Kong feels as 1997 approaches, and power is handed back to the mainland Chinese. These charges are not without cause, since much of the complex plotting of *Once Upon a Time in China* (which is now a series of five films) involves political intrigue, much of it concerning the influence of foreign powers on China. But whatever motivated the making of the film, it remains a monumental piece of work. With Jet Li, Rosamund Kwan, Yuen Biao. Directed By Tsui Hark. 1992.

People's Hero

At first glance a virtual remake of *Dog Day Afternoon, People's Hero* is anything but a slavish duplicate. It takes the basic melody of the original movie and then improvises a dozen terrific different jazzy riffs. At the heart of the movie is a towering performance by Ti Lung (a '60s and '70s kung fu movie star who made a spectacular comeback in John Woo's *A Better Tomorrow*). He plays a small-time gangster who just happens to be in the bank as it's being robbed by a couple of bumbling youths. Trapped inside with the robbers and employees, he seizes the opportunity to exploit the situation and negotiate himself and his incarcerated girlfriend a ticket out of HK. It's a tense, beautifully modulated movie and, unlike many HK films, the emphasis is on character rather than spectacle. With Ti Lung, Tony Leung and Ti Lung. Directed by Yee Tungshing. 1987.—Tod Booth

Rouge

Anita Mui stars as a long-suffering ghost in Stanley Kwan's bittersweet *Rouge*.

Ghosts are a popular subject in HK cinema, most often employed in kooky comedies, spooky period films, or some hybrid combo of the two. Director Stanley Kwan has something very different in mind. Winner of 3 Golden Horse Awards (Taiwan's "Oscar"), *Rouge* is sensuous and melancholy film about a beautiful ghost (Anita Mui, a hugely popular singer/film star in Asia) searching for her lost lover in modern Hong Kong. They committed suicide together 50 years previously, intending to spend eternity together in Hell rather than be separated by his disapproving parents (she worked in a brothel). But when "Master 12" fails to show up in Hell, Fleur returns to Earth to find him. She befriends a yuppie couple who epitomize the "80s relationship"—cool, independent, uncommitted. Fascinated by her archaic clothes, language, and otherworldly manner, they accept her ghostness with little trouble and agree to help in her quest. *Rouge* slips back and forth in time, contrasting the

sumptuous brothels and theaters of 1936 Hong Kong with the stark, neon, de-historicized city of today, creating a richly textured look at what David Chute in *Film Comment* calls, "the ways in which the past haunts the present in a city like history-heavy Hong Kong." With Anita Mui, Leslie Cheung, Alex Law. Directed by Stanley Kwan. 1987.—Tod Booth

Zu: Warriors of the Magic Mountain

This is one of the Hong Kong fantasy films that first made Westerners sit up and bark. Saying that this epic-scale tale of good and evil spirits, demons, warriors and the possible end of the world is over-the-top is like saying the Sahara could use a refreshment stand. The warriors in this film dance, leap, cartwheel, and use their swords as springboards. Monks, both good and bad, seldom walk; they've been meditating and perfecting themselves for so long that they've learned to fly. *Zu: Warriors of the Magic Mountain*, in fact, is notorious for having pretty much created the "wire work" movie genre—an action film where actors are suspended on invisible wires. Instead of ordinary displays of martial arts, they bounce off walls, statues, roofs, and each other while displaying their fighting skills. You will not be edified by *Zu: Warriors of the Magic Mountain*, but you will have a wonderful time watching it. With Yuen Biao and Samo Hung. Directed By Tsui Hark. 1983.

Monks and demons fly and battle in midair in Tsui Hark's ground-breaking fantasy, *Zu: Warriors of the Magic Mountain*.

Other-worldly beauty and action make *A Chinese Ghost Story* **a must-see Hong Kong film.**

A Chinese Ghost Story

Visually lush and exciting to watch, *A Chinese Ghost Story* combines eroticism, horror, comedy, action, and swordplay into a film that's a modern Hong Kong classic. Produced by the prolific and influential producer/director Tsui Hark, *A Chinese Ghost Story* is a simple story told in a gleeful, though seamless style. An innocent traveling scholar/tax collector meets and falls in love with the ghost of a beautiful young woman. The ghost is in the control of a nasty and matronly tree spirit who uses her to seduce and suck the life from mortal men. When the young man learns that the object of his affection is a ghost, he's at first shocked, but then tries to help her escape from the tree demon. His attempts get him into all sorts of trouble, from bumping into some particularly slow and stupid zombies to fighting a ghost army on the plains of Hell. This is a physically gorgeous film, making wonderful use of lighting, color, and slow-motion to heighten the beauty and otherworldliness of the tale. A must-see for anyone's Hong Kong list. With Joey Wong and Leslie Cheung. Directed By Ching Siu Tung. 1987.

Hong Kong Video Sources

Far East Flix catalog $3 from: Far East Flix, 59-13 68th Ave., Ridgewood, N.Y. 11385; voice/fax 718-381-6757 (Mon-Sat 11 a.m. to 7 p.m.)

Jars Video Collectibles catalog $4 from: Jars Video Collectibles, P.O. Box 113, Little Neck, NY 11363; 718-456-0663 (call from 7:30 a.m. to 10:30 p.m. only)

Older kung fu and recent Chinese videos, straight from Hong Kong, including some rare titles.

Laser Island catalog $10 from: Laser Island, 1810 Voorhies Ave., Brooklyn, NY 11235; 718-743-2425; fax 212-582-2634

Japanese laser discs, which include many HK titles. Also a wide selection of quality mainstream drama, musicals, kid movies, etc.

Spinning Tales catalog $15/6 issues ($19 Canada; $23.10 overseas) from: Laser Island, 1810 Voorhies Ave., Brooklyn, NY 11235; 718-743-2425; fax 212-582-2634

Laser disc newsletter from Laser Island; new domestic and import titles, plus ratings of laser transfers, etc.

Tai Seng catalog free from: Tai Seng, 170 Spruce Ave., #200, South San Francisco, CA 94080; 415-871-8118; 415-871-2392

High-quality Chinese videos, from action to romance. Good quality covers and video transfers make Tai Seng the best HK-based video company operating in the U.S.

Threat Theatre International catalog $10/6 issues (also 10% discount on all videos) from: Threat Theatre, P.O. Box 7633, Olympia, WA 98507; 206-352-3752

Good quality gray market prints of hard-to-find HK titles. They tend toward action, gore, sex, and comedy, but have a good selection of quality HK, too, most of which is letterboxed. Also Euro-porn and cult videos.

Video Search of Miami catalog free from: Video Search of Miami, P.O. Box 16-1917, Miami, FL 33166; 305-279-9773

Amazingly wide selection of hard-to-find Hong Kong and Japanese films. One caution: the quality of individual titles varies greatly. Some are pristine, while others are murky and muddy. They also carry rare Italian and Euro-trash titles, as well as out-of-circulation U.S. videos.

Hong Kong Video Zines

Asian Eye

$7/issue ($5 in Canada; make check payable to Colin Geddes) from: Asian Eye, 253 College Street #108, Toronto, Ontario, Canada M5T 1R5

Hong Kong Film Monthly

$15/6 issues ($30/12 issues) from: HKFM, 601 Van Ness Ave., #E3728, San Francisco, CA 94102

Cineraider

$12/3 issues ($18 foreign; make check payable to Richard Akiyama) from: Richard Akiyama, P.O. Box 240226, Honolulu, HI 96824-0226

Asian Trash Cinema

$20/year (4 issues; $6 sample copy) from: Asian Trash Cinema, P.O. Box 5367, Kingwood, TX 77325

ATC has published a book with 700 Asian film reviews, lots of photos, plus actor and director info. A good start for any novice. The book is $22.85 postpaid from the above address.

Oriental Cinema

$6/issue from: Damon Foster, P.O. Box 576, Fremont, CA 94537-0576

Martial Arts Movie Associates

$10/year (4 issues; $15 foreign) from: William Connolly, 6635 De Longpre #4, Hollywood, CA 90028

Hong Kong Movie Posters

Dragon Art catalog free (with SASE) from: Dragon Art, P.O. Box 9307, N. Hollywood, CA 91609; 818-766-3062

Posters from popular Hong Kong flicks: Jackie Chan, John Woo, *Heroic Trio, Once Upon A Time In China, Swordsman* series, *Black Cat, Eastern Condors,* etc. Depending on condition, posters are priced anywhere from $15 to $50. They also carry lobby cards in singles and sets. Also some zines and cult movie posters.

JAPANIMATION

Battle Angel

$39.45 ppd (TX residents add sales tax) from: A.D. Vision, 2709 Chimney Rock Rd., Houston, TX 77056; 713-965-0886

Battle Angel is a stylish and colorful mystery set in a future in which mutants and cyborgs are commonplace sights. In part one, we find Ido, a cyborg tech/doctor, coming across the remains of a young female cyborg in a junk yard. He brings her home, reconstructs her, and names her Gally, treating her as his daughter. Ido isn't the only cyborg doctor in the city. A female friend, Chiren, also rebuilds cyborgs, only she specializes in combat models for the gladiator-style entertainment everyone seems to watch.

People in general, and young women in particular, have to be careful in this city of the future. Not only are the night streets home to cerebellum-devouring "brain junkies," but blackmarketeers, too. One of the key components in creating a cyborg—the nerve endings in the human spinal column—is hard to duplicate. It's easier to kill someone and just steal his or her spine. And people do. Including Gally's sort of boyfriend. But Gally's pal isn't the only one with another side; virtually every character in *Battle Angel* has a secret identity and life. Ido hunts rogue cyborgs at night, Chiren hangs out with mobsters, even Gally finds a secret side to her own personality. When she's angered or physically threatened, her strength magnifies many times, and she fights with a skill that she has no right to possess. Clearly, she was something very different before she ended up in the junkyard, but what?

Bubblegum Crisis

video $27.95; laserdisc $42.95 ppd each (NC residents add sales tax) from: AnimEigo, P.O. Box 989, Wilmington, NC 28402; 910-251-1850; Fax 910-763-2376; email 72447.37@compuserve.com

The 8-part *Bubblegum Crisis* series is so popular that it's spawned a series of ersatz-concert videos. That's right; not since The Archies have you had a chance to watch a cartoon, and shake your booty to their hit records as well.

The series stars Priss, pop singer, and her gal pals Sylia, Linna, and Nene, a cop. Of course, when they're not being pop stars, aerobics instructors, cops, and fashion designers, they're superheroes. In their robotic battle armor, they become the Knight Sabers, a bunch of freelance, robot smashing vigilantes. Their targets are Boomers, illegal cyborgs who have a habit of using their heavy weapons on Tokyo's citizens and buildings.

What makes *Bubblegum Crisis* is the high-level animation pushing along the rock video-like combo of action and music. This isn't the grotesque violence of *Urotsukidoji* or *Fist of the North Star,* but the fun-for-the-whole-family violence of adolescent superhero dreams. When it's combined with the glitzy fashions and music score, the effect is like looking at an artifact from another planet.

Besides the 8-part series, there are two *Bubblegum Crisis* rock video compilations available, *Hurricane Live 2032,* and *Hurricane Live 2033-Tinsel City Rhapsody,* consisting of edited footage from the series with original segments.

Twilight of the Cockroaches

$33.95 ppd (CA residents add sales tax) from: Streamline Pictures, P.O. Box 691418, W. Hollywood, CA 90069; 310-998-0070; fax 310-998-1145

A strange little film that mixes live action with animation. The most unusual quality of the movie is that it's told from the point of view of all-too-human looking cockroaches. From the bugs' vantage point, humans are the source of food, and monsters to be feared. These roaches live in and around the kitchen of a bachelor gourmet who's constantly bringing home exotic cuisine from India, Morocco, and France. The roaches are portrayed as rather civilized, trapped in a never-ending cycle of battle with their human host. *Twilight of the Cockroaches* has been called a cross between Kafka and *Roger Rabbit,* and that's not a bad description.

Fist of the North Star

$33.95 ppd (CA residents add sales tax) from: Streamline Pictures, P.O. Box 691418, W. Hollywood, CA 90069; 310-998-0070; fax 310-998-1145

Both the good and the bad guys in *Fist of the North Star* are so much larger than life, they make Hulk Hogan look like Pee Wee Herman. The setting is a medieval future following a nuclear war. The story follows a number of characters, some of whom are trying to rebuild the devastated world, while others are battling over the woman they both want. It's this last story that gets the most screen time, and why not? The characters were probably more interesting to draw; they're certainly interesting to watch.

Chin and Ken are the Fists of the South and North Stars, respectively—warrior clans who keep order in their regions. They both love Julia, a suitably kind-hearted and fair-haired cartoon love interest. What makes all this interesting is the way Chin, Ken, and the other warrior characters settle their differences. They fight, but not in any way you've seen before. Their advanced martial arts skills allow them to crush skulls with one hand and literally tear each other limb from limb (all in glorious slow-motion). When that's not enough, they'll lop off part of a mountain and drop it on their opponent. *Fist of the North Star* is a hot mix of *Road Warrior* imagery crossed with samurai legends.

Project A-ko

video $33.99; laserdisc $43.99 ppd each (NY residents add sales tax) from: Central Park Media, 250 W. 57th St., #831, NY, NY 10107; 800-626-4277

Project A-ko combines, parodies, and celebrates many different Japanimation styles and themes. It's set at the Graviton High School for Girls, in which A-ko and her little pal C-ko are new students. Another student, B-ko, falls hard for C-ko. A-ko, however, isn't letting her friend go easily, so the two girls battle it out. What sets this battle apart from some after-school special is that A-ko has superhuman strength. She just does, trust me. B-ko, on the other hand, has access not only to other, larger girl students (some of whom look disturbingly like a paler Hulk), but a seemingly endless supply of Transformer-like robot battle suits. She and her hench-girls duke it out superhero-style with A-ko in the school yard. And did I mention that there is an alien spaceship heading for earth?

Robot Carnival

$33.95 ppd (CA residents add sales tax) from: Streamline Pictures, P.O. Box 691418, W. Hollywood, CA 90069; 310-998-0070; fax 310-998-1145

Robot Carnival is a wall-to-wall eyeball feast, starting with opening credits. It's a finely controlled sequence of comedy, grace, and mayhem as the words ROBOT CARNIVAL, themselves a city-sized robot, smash their way through the town they're supposed to entertain.

Other highlights include a sequence titled "Cloud," which shows a robot's life-journey in painterly pastoral and apocalyptic images. "Presence" is the strange and melancholy story of a man who never quite grows up, and decides to create the perfect female robot. The animators use images of time and the robot-builder's imagination to exquisite effect. "A Tale of Two Robots" is the imaginative and satirical tale of a battle between two huge steam-driven Transformer-style robots in the 19th century. "Nightmare" is a wild, post-apocalyptic "Sorcerer's Apprentice" in the ruins of a dead city. *Robot Carnival* is a terrific sampler of Japanese animation styles, from realistic to stylized, from funny to somber.

Speed Racer

$10.20 ppd (WA residents add sales tax) from: Whole Toon Catalog, P.O. Box 369, Issaquah, WA 98027-0369; 206-441-4130; fax 206-441-4295

The Summer of Love brought America something besides beads, free love, and electric Kool-Aid—it brought *Speed Racer* to U.S. television! Originally titled the much cooler *Mach Go, Go, Go* in Japan, the lead character in the series was the car itself, with the people playing second fiddle. Trans-Lux bought the English-language rights and, in a smart move by the Japanese production company that created the series, part of their contract specified that the music had to remain intact in the American version. Only the words to the songs (and dialog of the shows) were changed, and even that stuck as closely as possible to the original Japanese versions. What we ended up with was one of the most popular Japanese animated series in American TV history, and one of the best TV theme songs of all time. *Go Speed Racer, Go!*

Wicked City

$25 ppd from: Threat Theatre, P.O. Box 7633, Olympia, WA 98507;
206-352-3752

While not an official release in the U.S., this unsubtitled gray market
print of *Wicked City* (aka *Supernatural Beast City*) is well worth
checking out for its visuals alone. Like *Urotsukidoji* (though not as
sexually grotesque), this is another film in which the animators
unhinged their imaginations and libidos, letting them float free. The
story concerns an attempted mutant takeover of Tokyo (different
translations have so far given different explanations of the mutants'
origins). The opening encounter between a would-be john and a
prostitute is eerily horrifying and erotic. During sex, the hooker
slowly transforms into a woman-spider: her arms and legs distend
into hinged insect-like limbs, while retaining their human covering.
The woman's face remains unchanged, and her spider movements
are so smooth and sleek that even transformed, she remains attractive. This scene is also a classic—and scary—vagina dentata
sequence that's not to be missed.

While losing something without the subtitles, *Wicked City* remains
enough of a visual feast to justify watching the images and making
up your own dialog.

Grave of the Fireflies

video $43.95; laserdisc $43.99 ppd each (NY residents add sales tax)
from: Central Park Media, 250 W. 57th St., #831, NY, NY 10107;
800-626-4277

Grave of the Fireflies stands far apart from the other titles in this section. It's a serious, somber, even grim portrait of life in Japan weeks
before the American occupation. The land and people are devastated. It's through this landscape that we follow 14-year-old Seita
and 4-year-old Setsuko, an orphaned brother and sister who come
out of the abandoned bomb shelter where they live to desperately
search for food and water. While this might not sound like the subject for a cartoon, the story is well written, realistic, and well animated. And like Japan itself, which eventually emerged from its wreck-
age, *Grave of the Fireflies* finally gives viewers a glimpse of hope in
what is otherwise a disturbing and very adult cartoon about kids.

Urotsukidoji:
Legend of the Overfiend

$43.95 ppd (NY residents add sales tax) from: Central Park Media, 250 W. 57th St., #831, NY, NY 10107; 800-626-4277

Straight out of the violence-and-libido-heavy world of *manga* (Japanese comic books), the most extreme Japanese cartoons set the not-necessarily-psychologically-healthy standard when it comes to slamming eye-popping images and undigested sexual fantasies up on the screen.

The plot of *Urotsukidoji: Legend of the Overfiend* is basic, a simple engine to move the characters around: every 3,000 years the Overfiend tries to unite the three cosmic dimensions: Humans, Man Beasts, and Demons. Now the Overfiend wants to destroy them, bringing the entire universe to an end. The only one who can stop him is a half-human, half-magical teenager who looks like a cross between an alley cat and a high school football team towel boy. Got that?

Like a lot of adult Japanimation, *Urotsukidoji* is a mix of images and ideas lifted from science fiction, fantasy, horror movies, and soft-core porn. The fix you get in this video is not the story, but the style. *Urotsukidoji* is told through the eyes of desperately horny teeny-boppers and superbeings. The film is full of skyscraper-sized demons (brandishing their genitals like Tomahawk missiles), bizarre landscapes, and transdimensional beasts bursting from the skins of alluring humans—a mass of slimy tentacles and glowing monster sex secretions. A half-hour of *Urotsukidoji* would have Freud on the carpet, gibbering like an electro-shocked baboon.

For the truly damaged, note that *Urotsukidoji: Legend of the Overfiend* is an English-language-dubbed, 90-minute version of a more elaborate, over six-hour version of the Overfiend story. So far, the longer version is spread over five separate tapes (also available from Central Park Media). The longer version uses subtitles, and is not dubbed. It is also uncut, so all the most gruesome violence and sexual details are left moistly intact.

Japanimation Sources

A.D. Vision catalog free from: A.D. Vision, 2709 Chimney Rock Rd., Houston, TX 77056; 713-965-0886

Anime, original, and reprint comics; videos include *Devil Hunter Yohko, Sol Bianaca* and *Battle Angel*; their SoftCel series is for Japanese adult (i.e., sex-oriented) titles.

AnimEigo catalog free from: AnimEigo, P.O. Box 989, Wilmington, NC 28402; 910-251-1850; Fax 910-763-2376; email 72447.37@compuserve.com

Huge selection of quality Anime, including the *Bubblegum Crisis* series, and *Madox-01,* a parody of all those "armored suit" cartoons.

Art-Toons catalog free from: Art-Toons, P.O. Box 600, Northfield, OH 44067; 216-468-2655

Anime, plus American TV toons, Disney, MGM, Warner Bros., commercials, etc.

J.A.R.S. Video catalog $4 from: J.A.R.S. Video Collectibles, Attn: Joseph Ragus Sr., P.O. Box 113, Little Neck, NY 11363; 718-456-0663

Specializes in Hong Kong cinema, but they have a Japanimation supplement to their regular catalog.

The Right Stuf catalog free from: The Right Stuf, P.O. Box 71309, Des Moines, IA 50325-1309; 800-338-6827; fax 515-279-7434

Great animation from Japanese TV: *Astroboy, Gigantor, The Eighth Man,* etc. Plus T-shirts, posters, and books.

Streamline Pictures catalog free from: Streamline Pictures, P.O. Box 691418, W. Hollywood, CA 90069; 310-998-0070; fax 310-998-1145

Akira and series like *Crying Freeman* and *Dirty Pair,* plus vintage American TV animations, posters, CDs, etc.

Tunes Sound & Vision newsletter free from: Tunes Sound & Vision, 1200-TS. Air Depot, Midwest City, OK 73110; 405-733-5066

Broad selection of Anime titles; send your name and address and ask to be put on the Japanimation mailing list.

U.S. Manga catalog free from: Central Park Media, 250 W. 57th St., #831, NY, NY 10107; 800-626-4277

Probably the company with the biggest selection of Japanimation titles. They also specialize in adult (i.e., grittier and more violent) versions of popular Japanese titles, such as *The Guyver* series.

Whole Toon Catalog catalog $2 from: Whole Toon Catalog, 1907 3rd Ave., Seattle, WA 98101; 206-441-4130

Cartoons! Featuring intense Japanese adventure toons, *Flintstones, Ren & Stimpy,* Disney, etc. Cartoon-related toys, and some laserdiscs, too.

Animation Zines

Animag information from: Malibu Graphics, 5321 Sterling Center Dr., Westlake Village, CA 91361

Quarterly zine covering Japanimation in the U.S. and Japan itself. Also information on products, conventions, etc.

Animation Magazine $21/6 issues ($30 Canada; $39 overseas) from: Animation Magazine, 5889 Kanan Rd., #317, Agoura Hills, CA 91301

A slick, animation zine looking at mostly mainstream TV and film animation (*Beavis & Butthead, Ren & Stimpy,* Disney, *X Men,* etc.), with Japanimation on occasion.

Wild Cartoon Kingdom information from: LFP, 9171 Wilshire Blvd., #300, Beverly Hills, CA 90210

TV toons, stop-motion animation, and Japanimation. Lots of great graphics.

Japanese Models and Toys

Heroes Club, 840 Clement St., San Francisco, CA 94118; 415-387-4552; fax 415-387-5229

No catalog available, but they get regular shipments from Japan. Call or write (send SASE) with requests.

Inteleg Int'l. catalog free with SASE from: Inteleg Int'l., 354 W. Lancaster Ave., #220, Haverford, PA 19041; 215-896-8177; fax 215-896-1745

Official distributor of MAX Factory model kits in the U.S.

JAM Inc. catalog $3 from: JAM Inc., Rt. 1, P.O. Box 742, Brogue, PA 17309; 800-851-8309; 717-927-9787; fax 717-927-6538

Japanese models kits, including soft vinyl and plastic kits, from Anime and even live-action shows like *Kamen Rider, Solbrain,* also *Super Deformed Gundam,* etc.

Kimono My House catalog $2 from: Kimono My House, 1424 62nd St., Emeryville, CA 94608; 510-654-4627; fax 510-654-4621

A broad selection of Japanese videos, model kits, t-shirts, toys, etc.

Art Meets Science and Spirituality in a Changing Economy

$34.90 each; $136.90 series ppd (CA, NY, MI, CT residents add sales tax) from: Mystic Fire Video, P.O. Box 2249, Livonia, MI 48151; 800-292-9001; 313-416-8203

Anyone who has seen the video discussions between Bill Moyers and Joseph Campbell (also distributed by Mystic Fire) will have some idea of the fascination and contradictions in a video series of this sort—a succession of talking heads that instead of boring you, deliver hours of synapse-popping ideas and discussions.

In 1990 artists Joseph Beuys and Robert Filliou gathered a group of scientists, artists, spiritual leaders, and economists in Amsterdam for a five-day conference to hash over the possibility of a truly holistic world view and its implications for the future of the world economy— basically, how to make sure the machine doesn't fall apart, and make it run better in the future. Some of the series participants include Rupert Sheldrake, Fritjof Capra, Marina Abramovic, Ilya Prigogine, and John Cage.

This five-part video series which grew out of the conference combines highlights from panel discussions with follow-up interviews, allowing many of the speakers to expand on their ideas. But what really makes the series fascinating is the combination of thinkers in each episode. On the very first tape you have group and individual discussions wherein the Dalai Lama talks about the true nature of the mind, and the plight of the Tibetan people, Robert Rauschenberg describes working with natural processes in his art, David Bohm talks about his search for the "implicate order" of the universe, and Russian economist Stanislav Menshikov looks at the economic implications of a holistic worldview.

The Dalai Lama discusses the true nature of the human mind in the first episode of *Art Meets Science and Spirituality in a Changing Economy.*

One of the most rewarding aspects of a series like this is that it's impossible to absorb all of it in a single viewing—each tape is as information-dense as a book. And like a good book, this is the kind of series that can open your mind and change your point of view.

The Baby Cart series

$27.90 ppd each from: Video Search of Miami, P.O. Box 16-1917, Miami, FL 33166; 305-279-9773

They're known in different places as the *Sword of Vengeance* series, *Lone Wolf and Cub,* and the *Baby Cart* films. This last name comes from the ramshackle buggy in which Itto Ogami, a *ronin* (a wandering, masterless samurai) pushes his three-year-old son. Originally released in the U.S. in 1974 and 1981 as *Lightning Swords of Death* and *Shogun Assassin* respectively, these U.S. films were pieced together from several of the original six-part Japanese series. Even in truncated versions, these tales of a samurai forced to become a freelance assassin captured a following for their images of the relentlessly stoic swordsman, his son, and for what Leonard Maltin called their "stunning visual ballet of violence and bloodletting."

The Japanese videos and laserdiscs have been available from import houses, but they typically cost hundreds of dollars and worse, were non-subtitled. For some action films, this doesn't matter, but for films so steeped in Japanese tradition and myth, the meaning of these stories was virtually deleted without subtitles. Now for the first time, you can find all six of the original *Baby Cart* films subtitled in English, and in letterbox format (so that you get the original widescreen image, and so the subtitles don't run off the edges of the screen). Video Search of Miami, a gray market video sales club, who subtitled the films themselves, deserve a big thank you from all fans of action cinema, Japanese, and foreign films.

Bittersweet: A True Love Story

$34.95 ppd (CA residents add sales tax) from: House 'O Chicks, 2215-R Market St., #813, San Francisco, CA 94114; 415-861-9849

It's funny to start off a review of an s/m dyke porn video by saying that the most shocking thing in it is a kiss, but it's true. *Bittersweet* follows a dominatrix as she returns home from "a hard day of work at the dungeon." After a candlelight bath, she dresses in corset and boots, before she and her submissive partner play—safely—with piercing, flagellation, and fisting.

Visually, *Bittersweet* is impressive and evocative, with the grainy video texture enhancing the images. The film foregoes dialog, and instead has a soundtrack of what you might have to call "women's music." Those who find this distracting can hit the mute button and provide their own soundtrack, but will miss the crack of the whip and other sounds.

At the end of the film the two actresses, Gabrielle and Michaela, share a kiss that's caring, tender and—almost unheard of in porn—genuine. Sincere and intimate, this kiss is the guarantee that what you've seen is the "true love story" of the title. —Daphne Gottlieb

The Brothers Quay, Vols. 1 & 2

video: $33.95 ppd (Canada/Mexico $35.95; Europe $36.95; Asia $41.95) from: First Run Features, 153 Waverly Place, NY, NY 10014; 800-229-8575; laserdisc: information from: The Voyager Co., Customer Service Dept., 1 Bridge St., Irvington, NY 10533; 800-446-2001

The Brothers Quay are American twins living in London who periodically send out short film dispatches from the far side of their collective unconsciouses. The best of their work, such as the *Street of Crocodiles* and *Rehearsals for Extinct Anatomies,* combine sort of

Freud-on-acid imagery with storylines by Kafka. Imagine the Muppets as directed by Dali or Buñuel.

The majority of the Quays' work is stop motion animation—a technique where artists move models or objects a fraction of an inch, photograph them, and then move them again, until the final result looks like natural motion on film. Unlike many other animators, however, in the Quays' world any object in the film frame has an equal chance of becoming an actor. In the *Street of Crocodiles* for instance, the detritus in a broken-down tailor shop—straight pins, a child's toys, dressing dummies, the rusted screws in the floor—come to fantastic and grotesque life, tormenting the tailor and delighting his son. It's this splicing of the organic world with the inorganic that creates much of the surreal tension in the brothers' work. Often in the films, as inanimate objects spring to life, they're as curious about us as we are about them.

The Brothers Quay, animators of dreams and nightmares.

Daddy and the Muscle Academy

The Art, Life and Times of Tom of Finland

$55.95 ppd (CA residents add sales tax) from: Tom of Finland Co., Dept. CCS, P.O. Box 26716, Los Angeles, CA 90026; 800-334-6526; outside U.S. 213-250-1685; fax 213-481-2092

The Leather Daddy. The Marlboro Cowboy. The Motorcycle Officer. The Sailor. Although today these images of gay male sexuality are familiar, this is in no small part due to the art of Tom of Finland. From his early drawings of buffed-out boys to his later, nastier work, Tom's drawings transcended under-the-bed reading and were instrumental in the making of many a leatherman.

Containing a series of interviews completed shortly before his death, the film features Tom narrating his career, giving insight into his iconography and biography. His voice is joined by those of "Tom's men," who found his work formative to their fantasies, identities and sexualities. Well-made, entertaining, and filled with hot men, *Daddy and the Muscle Academy* is a 55-minute love note to one of the (ahem) seminal figures of gay male culture as we know it.—Daphne Gottlieb

Erotica SF

$34.95 ($39.95 foreign) postpaid from: Oranj Productions, 499 Alabama St., #307, San Francisco, CA 94110; 415-861-4101

Erotica SF was a cable interview show that profiled both sex workers and sexy people, mostly in the San Francisco area. Its host was the lovely Madeleine. *Erotica SF* has all the immediacy and goofiness of any public access cable show. This one, however, was a little too hot for Viacom, the local cable company, and they pulled the plug on the show. Even when it was being broadcast, however, Viacom censored the shows, which meant home viewers could listen to panting voices and giggles while watching a blank screen. This video version of *Erotica SF* features four uncensored half-hour episodes, with lots of bonus footage: outtakes that Madeleine knew would never make it on mainstream cable, such as performance artist Linda Serbu doing a monologue about sex work while being fisted. There is also a discussion about proper cunt shaving techniques with Nina Hartley. The tape also includes the charming short film "Hi Mom," shot during the San Francisco Gay and Lesbian parade.

There are lots more *Erotica SF* video titles on the way. For a catalog, send $1 to the address above.

Polyester

information from: The Voyager Co., Customer Service Dept., 1 Bridge St., Irvington, NY 10533; 800-446-2001

John Waters' film *Polyester;* now released on laserdisc, brings together both the Capraesque and huckster parts of his work. In *Polyester,* the late Divine plays a big and beautiful housewife who is driven to drink and despair by an abusive husband, a heavy-metal bad-girl daughter, and a son who is a psycho foot-fetishist. Divine is trying desperately to hold her family together. Into all this mess, Waters tosses an avaricious mother-in-law and Tab Hunter, the black-and-white-TV-era heart-throb who can still make the ladies cum just by smiling.

Divine and friends camp it up in one of the bonus archival stills from Voyager's laserdisc of John Waters' *Polyester.*

One element of *Polyester* that shows Waters' exploitation roots isn't just in the film (or in this case, laserdisc). It's something you hold in your hand. *Polyester* uses a '50s-style B-movie gimmick that Waters invented: Odorama. Really, Odorama is just a scratch-and-sniff card with scented numbers that correspond to numbers that appear on the screen. Throughout the movie, whenever a character sniffs something a number flashes, and you can scratch away. Some of the smells are pleasant. Some smells...aren't.

Voyager has lovingly reproduced copies of the original Odorama cards for this laserdisc package to give you the total *Polyester* experience. Also included in the package are a special audio track with Waters' commentary on the film and a selection of his briefer works, including his legendary "No Smoking" theatrical short.

Peeping Tom

information from: The Voyager Co., Customer Service Dept., 1 Bridge St., Irvington, NY 10533; 800-446-2001

Long before slasher flicks like *Halloween*, Michael Powell created a sexual horror film that thrust the filmgoer into the killer's point of view. On this newly released laserdisc version of the film, Karl Boehm plays Mark, a photographer who has a side job shooting "nudie" photos. Mark's clandestine porn biz brings him into contact with a lot of women's bodies. He develops a fascination with physical imperfection, and documents his obsession by filming his models as he murders them. Powell uses the camera as a weapon, showing us Mark's attacks from his point of view through the camera lens right into the faces of his victims. *Peeping Tom* is a movie about voyeurism; it asks questions about the role of both filmmaker and viewers in creating the world that's depicted on the screen. This isn't a sexy movie. You won't get turned on by its '60s nudie layouts, 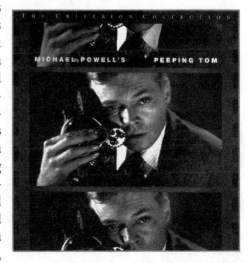 but as a film that looks at both sex and obsession in an honest and intelligent way, *Peeping Tom* was way ahead of its time.

Hemo the Magnificent

$12.95 ppd (CA residents add sales tax) from: Rhino Home Video, 2225 Colorado Ave., Santa Monica, CA 90404-3555; 800-843-3670

I first saw *Hemo the Magnificent,* an educational film on blood and how it circulates in your body, back in 1967 when I was in the seventh grade. When I watched it last night, I realized that I still could quote lines from the film verbatim. After all those years, I still remembered certain images—such as the footage of blood cells squeezing one by one through a tiny capillary and the animated sequence that explains your brain's control over blood flow.

The film begins with an argument between a balding scientist named "Dr. Research" and an animated character named Hemo. Their discussion of the mystery and origins of blood has a compelling drama, which isn't surprising if you know that this film was written, produced, and directed by Academy Award winner Frank Capra (*It's a Wonderful Life*). The animation is by Shamus Culhane of *Betty Boop* and *Snow White* fame.

Hemo the Magnificent is one of a series of educational films produced by Bell Laboratories back in the 1950s. I've talked to physicists who rave about *Our Mr. Sun,* another film in the same series. If you have any interest in scientific understanding of how the world works, these films are great resources.—Pat Murphy

Safe is Desire

$46.45 ppd (Canada $48.45; overseas $48.45; CA residents add sales tax) from: Fatale Video, 526 Castro St., San Francisco, CA 94114; 800-845-4617

A safe sex video with a difference; actually, a couple of them. First, it's aimed squarely at lesbians. Secondly, it's 99% "how to" free, and concentrates instead on showing that safe sex can be every bit as hot and twisted as unsafe sex. It's a little fable really—an attractive lesbian couple meet and are attracted to each other; in bed, though, one woman's insistence that they use dams and gloves startles her new lover completely out of the mood. They go for help, information, and encouragement to the wizard's castle which, in this case, is a women's sex club. After an inspiring evening of watching sweaty demos by The Safe Sex Sluts (not to mention some of the other club-goers), the reluctant half of our couple is convinced. She and her friend retire to bed where they delightedly (and safely) fuck like crazed weasels happily ever after.

After checking out *Safe is Desire,* I'm still left with the annoying question: So where the hell's a tape this hot for straight and bi couples?

Wild Wheels

$34.95 ppd (CA residents add sales tax; PAL version $44.95) from: Zoom In Productions, 10341 San Pablo Ave., El Cerrito, CA 94530

Some were inspired by dreams. Some were trying to fill long insomniac nights. Some are artists, others obsessive civilians. All of them have taken the most singular image of 20th-century America—the car—and made it wholly their own.

Wild Wheels looks at bizarrely decorated and modified cars, and the cars' owners. It's part fashion show, part travelogue, and part road story, as Harrold Blank (son of the famous documentary filmmaker, Les Blank) tools around the country and hangs out with car modifiers. The best moments are when Blank gets to the inner meaning the reformed vehicle has for its owner, such as Joe Gomez's story of seeing his wrought-iron VW Bug in a dream, and feeling the wind

"EXHILARATING!..."
If I were the education president, every kid and grown-up in America would have a WILD WHEELS tape. It's a movable feast!" —The News-Press

A film by Harrold Blank

blowing on him as he drove. Which isn't to say you should overlook vehicles like the visual pun: a bovine-shaped motorbike its owner calls a "Cowasaki."

This homemade "Cowasaki" is just one of the many artistic and bizarre vehicles featured in Harrold Blank's *Wild Wheels.*

Cars like the ones examined in *Wild Wheels* are psychological ciphers, bits of secret code coughed out by their owners' unconscious. The essence of the movie is sort of a pop culture version of the deciphering of the Rosetta Stone, only in *Wild Wheels,* we get lots of little Rosetta Stones, some moments of pathos and bizarre humor in the search.

The Wild, Wild World of Jayne Mansfield

$23 ppd (WA residents add sales tax; Canada/Mexico $25; overseas $27) from: Something Weird Video, P.O. Box 33664, Seattle, WA 98155; 206-361-3759

This is one of those remarkable films that 1) you've probably never heard of, and 2) could only have happened at a certain moment in time. *The Wild, Wild World of Jayne Mansfield* is just what it says it is, a peek inside the life of a movie star. And Mansfield is such a movie star, she's practically floating all over the screen, she's such a goddamn star. And she's brought along her pet Chihuahua, Choo-Choo. We're touring Europe with Jayne ("Rome, I love you!"), checking out nudist colonies, eating in smart restaurants with swinging international jetsetters, watching babes change from their work clothes to their evening gear in the bushes near the Coliseum in Rome. It's all so cool and carefree and groovy! *The Wild, Wild World of Jayne Mansfield* is a glimpse not only of a star and a practically extinct lifestyle, but it captures a wildly optimistic moment in time that seemed as if it would go on forever...

Girlfriends

information from: Riot Pictures, 216-246-6440

A cheesy, low budget exploitation romp with a lesbian serial-killing couple. Averse to "real" jobs, Wanda and Pearl collect food stamps and kill tricks for cash. Overblown characterizations border on the cartoon, including an s/m-switch serial killer, a racist white trash furniture salesman, and a community organizing lesbian feminist. Not over-the-top enough to be satire, but not good enough to reach the intended psychothriller status, *Girlfriends* is nonetheless 80 minutes of cultural bottom-feeding fun.—Daphne Gottlieb

Video Zines

Big Reel's Hollywood & Vine

free in U.S. (Canada $30/12 issues; overseas $60) from: Empire Publishing, P.O. Box 717, Madison, NC 27025; 919-427-5850; fax 919-427-7372

A tabloid newspaper featuring ads for film collectibles, everything from lobby cards and old films for a few bucks to ancient movie posters going for thousands.

Bright Lights Film Journal

$19.95/year (4 issues; $27.95 foreign) from: Bright Lights Film Journal, P.O. Box 420987, San Francisco, CA 94142-0987

A classy, smart, and attractive film zine that takes the high road in film scrutiny. Issue #12 focused on film noir, its history and continued effect on modern cinema. Also part one of a Fellini interview, the production history of Red Dust, and thoughtful reviews of videos, laserdiscs and books.

Bruce on a Stick

$12/year (4 issues; $16 foreign) from: Bruce on a Stick, P.O. Box 416, Tarrytown, NY 10591

The Bruce Campbell zine! Who's Bruce Campbell? Check out Evil Dead 1 & 2, and Brisco County Jr., and get back to me. (They cover some other cool trash movies, too.)

Cult Movies

$18/4 issues from: Cult Movies, 6201 Sunset Blvd., #152, Hollywood, CA 90028

Trash, horror, and cult cinema. Reviews, interviews with makers of classic horror and exploitation films. Lots of good graphics, including reproductions of film posters.

GV Guide

$14.95/year (6 issues; $23.95 foreign; make check payable to Sabin Publishing) from: Sabin Publishing, 7985 Santa Monica Blvd., #109-117, LA, CA 90046

A review, gossip and news zine covering gay (and a teeny bit of lesbian) porn videos. Interviews with stars, articles on "The Making Of..." letters and video contact info.

Scarlet Street

$18/year (4 issues; $4.95 sample) from: R.H. Enterprises, 271 Farrant Terrace, Teaneck, NJ 07666; 201-836-1113

"The Magazine of Mystery and Horror." Interviews and profiles of horror and mystery actors: Vincent Price, Ida Lupino, Bela Lugosi, Jeffrey Coombs, etc. Reviews of videos and audio recordings, comics and books; "Our Man On Baker Street," a column about TV and movies in the UK.

Tease!

$12/year (2 issues) from: Pure Imagination, 88 Lexington Ave., #2E, NY, NY 10016; 212-682-0025; fax 212-683-3664

From the fine humans who brought you The Betty Pages (the high-quality Betty Page zine), comes Tease!, a slick-paper zine that covers the other legends and babes of cheesecake photos and cinema. Great photo spreads, artist portfolios, interviews with vintage tease artists and contemporary exploitation artists, such as John Waters.

Video Watchdog Special Edition, #1

$7.95 ($12 foreign) from: Video Watchdog, P.O. Box 5283, Cincinnati, OH 45205-0283; 513-471-8989

From the folks who bring you the most obsessive film zine in the world, this is all the stuff they couldn't fit into a regular issue! All the usual info on different cuts and retitling on cult films, plus an interview with Euro-sexploitation director Walerian Borowczyk; lists of "Best of 1993" video and laser releases from obsessive film luminaries, a look at the slash and burn editing on Emmanuelle 5, plus Planeta Bur, the little known Russian SF film that was acquired by Roger Corman, chopped into pieces and pasted together to make a couple of U.S. schlock flicks. Plus, lots of video contact info, great ads and an index to the whole run of Video Watchdog.

Wrapped in Plastic

$25.50/year (6 issues; sample $3.95) from: Win-Mill Productions, 1912 E. Timberview Lane, Arlington, TX 76014; 817-274-7128

Obsessively fine **Twin Peaks**/David Lynch zine. Interviews include singer Julee Cruise, Frank Silva (Bob), Catherine Coulson (Log Lady), etc. Analysis of **TP**, info on **TP** actors, events and collectibles.

Sound and Vision

edited by S. Frith, A. Goodwin & L. Grossberg
$17.95; Routledge
1993; 215 pp.

Sound and Vision is one of the first books to look seriously at music videos as "one of the most important emergent cultural forms in contemporary popular culture." Ten essays lead you (occasionally turgidly) through the empire of signs, symbols, ideas and contradictions spawned by MTV and its colorful brood.

The Aesthetics of Ambivalence

by Brooks Landon
1992; 187 pp.
information from: Greenwood Press, 88 Post Road West, Westport, CT 06881; 203-226-3571

The Aesthetics of Ambivalence is an argument for reworking the way we judge science fiction films. Landon argues that SF movies and literature are different beasts, and that most SF film criticism continues to see film as an extension of literature, of narrative. To Landon, this misses the point, and he makes a good case for rethinking the way we look at filmed SF.

Offbeat Video Source Guide

by Dennis Murry
1994; 115 pp.
$19.95 ppd from: Offbeat Pub., 1972 NE Third St., #252, Bend, OR 97701

Not only is this the best non-library video sourcebook (i.e., it's under 25 lbs. and $200), it's a DIY classic. Using nothing more than an Apple IIE and his own obsessive need to write the book, Murry has created a comprehensive listing of virtually ever damned video distributor in the country, by category. Like the machine he wrote it on, the **Offbeat Video Source Guide** is primitive, but it works.

War and Cinema

by Paul Virilio
$17.95; Verso
1984; 95 pp.

Just as the autopsy is the important medical act of "seeing with one's own eyes," the act of seeing is so integral to warfare that vision and combat have evolved together. **War and Cinema** examines items such as the synchronized camera/machine guns on biplanes, and the close ties between the technologies of sight and the technologies of death.

Vampires and Violets

by Andrea Weiss
$12.50; Penguin Books
1992; 184 pp.

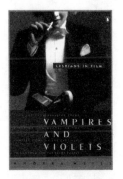

Andrea Weiss is a filmmaker and author of **Vampires and Violets**, an entertaining and informative look at lesbian characters in everything from art house flicks and exploitation pictures to mainstream movies such as *The Hunger* and *The Color Purple*. The danger of books like this is that they'll send you looking for such obscurities as Jean Rollin's *Le Viol des Vampires*, which is a compliment to both the author and her book.

Asian Trash Cinema: The Book

by Thomas Weisser
$22.85 ppd from: Asian Trash Cinema, P.O. Box 5367, Kingwood, TX 77325

Reviews of 600+ Asian pop films, mostly action, gangster, horror, and sex, with a little art thrown in. With its movie descriptions, director and genre indices, this is a fine reference book for the Hong Kong film novice. Like most books of its type, though, feel free to ignore its individual movie ratings.

Spaghetti Westerns

by Thomas Weisser
1992; 544 pp.
$47 ppd (NC residents add sales tax) from: McFarland & Co., P.O. Box 611 (Highway 88), Jefferson, NC 28640; 919-246-4460; fax 919-246-5018

A frighteningly thorough look at a rich and sometimes bizarre film genre that most dilettantes (like me) thought consisted of a maybe a few dozen films. **Spaghetti Westerns** contains a filmography of 558 Italian-made Westerns, with info on actors, directors, composers, writers, cinematographers, etc. This is another book that will send you back to the video store...

Alternative Filmworks, 259 Oakwood Ave., State College, PA 16803-1698; 800-797-3456; catalog free

Independent and experimental works on video. Short films, features, animation, etc.

Astral Oceans Cinema, P.O. Box 931753, Cherokee Ave., Hollywood, CA 90093; catalog $6 (must send statement that you are over 21)

Asian softcore and hardcore sexploitation, both live action and cartoons. Some Euro-porn and amateur sex tapes.

Atavistic Video, P.O. Box 578266, Chicago, IL 60657-8266; catalog free

Music videos by artists with an edge: Foetus, Diamanda Galas, Dream Syndicate, Pussy Galore, Killdozer, Laibach, Big Black, etc.

Discount Video Tapes, 833 "A" N. Hollywood Way, P.O. Box 7122, Burbank, CA 91510; 818-843-3366; fax 818-843-3821; catalog free

100s of tapes, all priced from $20 to $40. They also rent tapes by mail. The sample catalog has over 400 titles. The full catalog is $2, and contains over 2000 titles.

Drift Distribution, 219 E. 2nd St., #5E, NY, NY 10009; 212-254-4118; fax 212-254-3154; email: drift@well.sf.ca.us; catalog $2

Independent and experimental works on video. Short films, features, animation, etc.

Facets Video, 1517 W. Fullerton Ave., Chicago, IL 60614; 312-281-9075; 800-331-6197; catalog $9.95

Some of the best independent, foreign, art and instructional films available. Their huge catalog is like an encyclopedia of innovative video styles and subjects. Highlights include Larry Jordan's eccentric animations and James Broughton's very personal erotic short films. All of Facets' titles are for sale or rent.

Laser Flash, Sight & Sound, 27 Jones Rd., Waltham, MA 02154; 617-894-8633; fax 617-894-9329

New, used, and imported laserdiscs. Drama, comedy, Hong Kong, music, silent, and adult titles. Prices range from $15 (used disc) to $110 (import).

Mail Order Video, 7888 Ostrow St., #A, San Diego, CA 92111; 800-942-8273; fax 619-569-0505; catalog free

Military tactics and history, self-defense, "Sexy Girls and Sexy Guns," police procedures, gun, and knife info.

Milestone Film & Video, 275 W. 96th St., #28C, NY, NY 10025; 212-865-7449; fax 212-222-8952; catalog free

Lots of foreign and obscure titles. Pre-Revolutionary Russian cinema; travel videos from the '20s and '30s; animation tapes featuring Felix the Cat, and by artists Winsor McCay and Ladislaw Starewicz; also a few laserdiscs.

Tempe Video, P.O. Box 6573, Akron, OH 44312-0573; catalog free

Horror, slasher, zombie, and sexploitation specialists; many independent and hard-to-find titles.

Video Specialists Int'l, 182 Jackson St., Dallas, PA 18612; 717-675-0227

Old serials, silent films, vintage TV, westerns, horror, sexploitation.

Video Yesteryear, Box C, Sandy Hook, CT 06482; 800-243-0987; catalog $3

Silent films, drama, documentaries, westerns, serials, horror, vintage TV.

Visionary Communications, 28-30 The Square, St. Annes, Lytham, St. Annes FY8 1RF, England; 0253-712453; fax 0253-712362; catalog free with IRC

Mostly music videos of old and new Eurobands (Throbbing Gristle, Hawkwind, Alien Sex Fiend, Robyn Hitchcock). Also carry fetish, animation, gay/lesbian titles, a few weird classics (*Le Frisson de Vampire, Deep Red, Vampyr*).

The Voyager Co., 578 Broadway, NY, NY 10012; 800-446-2001; catalog free

Voyager is the killer laserdisc company. Their innovative Criterion series often includes extra material on the films: stills, storyboards, costume and set designs, etc. The series also features extra audio tracks with commentary by their directors and stars. Their titles cover such art house stalwarts as Fellini's *La Strada* and Robert Altman's *Secret Honor,* and cult favorites like John Waters' *Polyester* and John Woo's *The Killer.*

We Never Sleep, P.O. Box 92, Denver, CO 80201; fax 303-733-3480; catalog free

Experimental/noise/rock artists on video: Matt Heckert, The Haters, Survival Research Labs, Crash Worship. Also CDs, cassettes, LPs, and books.

TOOLS

Introduction—Tools

We define tools pretty broadly around here at Covert Culture World Headquarters. For us, a tool is pretty much anything you can use to make or do something else. A hammer is a tool; so is computer software; ideas are tools, too. Ideas are the tools we use to change our minds. An idea can be something you've carefully researched, or something you stumble on accidentally. It can lead you in new directions, and wrap up old ideas. You'll find some interesting ideas, and other tools, in this chapter's sections on UFOs, sex, and fashion. Some more prosaic, but no less interesting, tools are covered in CD-ROMs, pirate media (radio and TV hacking), software, and weapons. The Miscellaneous Tools section has both the idea-oriented and prosaic: *Schwa* kits (to help you through those alien abductions), *The Institute of Blinding Light* catalog (for all your heretical desires), *Where's the Art!!* (to feed your Elvis need), the Archie McPhee catalog (where you can find all those rubbers snakes and X-Ray specs you've been looking for), a **Twin Peaks** collectibles source, and on and on...

And don't forget that if ideas are tools, they still need people to spread them. So say something interesting to a stranger today. Nothing scary or threatening, just intriguing, such as "Aliens use my Cuisinart at night," or "If we had feet where our hands are, wouldn't gloves look funny?"

Blam!

for Macintosh; information from: The Voyager Co., Customer
Service Dept., 1 Bridge St., Irvington, NY 10533; 800-446-2001

How can you describe **Blam!** in mere words? It's sort of a CD-ROM
multimedia magazine. That's the nice way of putting it. It's also a
subversive, performance art, intertextual light/sound/picture/word
show. That's another way. **Blam!** is also a trip through a Jackson
Pollock-like brain after it's been high-jacked by some **Neuromancer**
bad guys, who pump it full of speed and ketamine and wire the
whole thing to a comsat so that everyone on the planet sees **Blam!**,
experiences **Blam!**, and is **Blam!** long enough to go stark, raving
bat-shit. I like it.

A Hard Day's Night

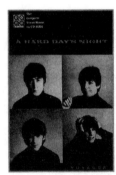

for Macintosh; information from: The Voyager Co., Customer
Service Dept., 1 Bridge St., Irvington, NY 10533; 800-446-2001
(Requirements: 25-MHz 68030 processor or better; System 6.0.7 or
later; 4MB RAM; 256 color or grayscale monitor; QuickTime-com-
patible CD-ROM drive)

The Voyager Company has always been at the leading edge of
laserdisc tech. Now they've opened the door on a whole new
film/disc medium: full-length theatrical films on CD-ROM. The first
release in this new series is The Beatles' *A Hard Day's Night* on both
Macintosh and DOS-compatible CD-ROMs.

You might expect Voyager to make a lot of compromises to fit a full-
length film onto a CD-sized disc, but that's not the case. Not only
do you get the full 90-minute *A Hard Day's Night*, but also the film
script, a selection of still photos, a theatrical trailer, an essay by film
historian Bruce Eder, an interview with the film's director, Richard
Lester, plus Lester's legendary short film, *The Running, Jumping and
Standing Still Film*. The CD-ROM version of the film is divided into
chapters, just like a regular laserdisc, allowing you to search and
replay your favorite scenes. There are also tools that let you "dog
ear" a section you want to refer back to, and a "notes" tool where
you can enter text. You can also choose from different playback formats. On the Macintosh version, you can choose between the the
QuickTime size for your monitor, or turn it into a screen-filling
double-sized version. If you're sitting at your computer, you'll prob-

A Hard Day's Night was the first rock 'n' roll movie that mattered to people who didn't particularly care about rock 'n' roll. The prologue, set to the song "I'll Cry Instead" – which was added to the film for its 1982 reissue – is evidence of just how seriously it is taken. What other rock 'n' roll movie was ever recut and lengthened for reissue 18 years after the fact?

FORMAT CONTENTS < MARK >
QUIT ? CONTROLS < FIND >   ◄ Commentary – 1 of 166 ►

ably want to use the smaller size, but choosing the larger image and moving back a few feet turns your monitor into a mini screening room for as many people as can crowd around (and people will definitely want to crowd around).

Creepy Crawlies

for IBM and clones; for information, call your local software outlet; in England, information from: MDI, The Old Hop Kiln, 1 Long Garden Walk, Farnham, Surrey, GU9 7HP; 0252-737630; fax 0252-710948 (Requirements: 80386 processor or better; 256 color VGA graphics card; MS-DOS 3.1 sound card)

Insects are the closet things to aliens most of us will ever experience. They have too many damned legs, wings, weird bodies and faces like some Lovecraftian feverdream. To better prepare yourself for alien encounters, I suggest picking up the info-packed **Creepy Crawlies**.

Not only do you get written information (in English or French) about 74 flying, crawling and jumping bugs from all over the world, but you get narrative description as well, with full-screen color images (you'll need nerves of steel for some of these) and full-motion video clips. The insects are grouped into "tours," which let you look at a lot of related insects at once. The tours include "Down to Earth" (ground insects), "Killers," "Pests" and "On the Wing" (flying insects). The disc is also indexed. Great for education, but I wouldn't show it to a kid too close to bedtime.

Freak Show

for Macintosh; information from: The Voyager Co., Customer Service Dept., 1 Bridge St., Irvington, NY 10533; 800-446-2001 (Requirements: 25-MHz 66030 processor or better; System 7.0; 5MB RAM; 13" color monitor; double-speed CD-ROM drive)

In these politically-aware and -correct times, carnival sideshows are pretty much ancient history. You might still be able to pay for a peek at a two-headed calf, but you're not going to get a glimpse of characters like Harry the Head, Wanda the Worm Woman, or Jelly Jack anywhere but on this disc courtesy of the performance group, The Residents.

Providing music, voices, and inspiration for the project, The Residents handed over the actual image-rendering to computer graphics whizz, Jim Ludke. He's created a netherworld landscape

that's part trailer park and part Gothic nightmare. You begin by wandering into the Freak Show tent, and choosing who you want to visit. But it's not that easy. The Freaks don't always want to answer your questions. The disc quickly becomes a kind of quest, as you try to track down the elusive freaks and get them to tell you their stories.

Glamour Girls of 1943

for Macintosh; information from: Space Coast Software, 3128 Lake Washington Rd., #244, Melbourne, FL 32934; 407-242-2040; fax 407-242-8682 (Requirements: 68020 processor or better; System 6.0.7 or later; 2.5MB RAM; 256 color or grayscale monitor)

The bulk of the **Glamour Girls of 1943** disc is taken up with surprisingly fetishistic images of '40s babes, sometimes nude and sometimes in panties and garter belts and occasionally wrestling. Though the photos themselves are G-rated by modern kink standards, the recurring images of wrestling, of elaborate underwear and of women with real bodies (i.e., ample hips and breasts) makes **Glamour Girls of 1943** a tasty pack of fetish eye-candy.

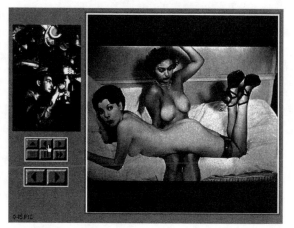

Mars Explorer

for IBM and clones; $125; Virtual Reality Laboratories, 2341 Ganador Court, San Luis Obispo, CA 93401; 805-545-8515; fax 805-781-2259 (Requirements: 80386 or 80486 processor; 4 MB RAM; MCGA, VGA or Super VGA graphics card; MS-DOS 3.0 or higher; Microsoft compatible mouse and driver; CD-ROM drive and software)

Even if human spaceflight makes little scientific sense, the romance of it is bred into the American consciousness; it's especially compelling for those of us who grew up during the height of the Space Age. In the sullen '90s, though, we know there's little chance of most of us even going into space. For those who grew up with dreams of interplanetary flight, the **Mars Explorer** CD-ROM is probably the next best thing.

Using images pieced together from NASA's Viking photos, **Mars Explorer** lets you scan the entire Martian surface in high and low resolution, from 52 degrees north latitude to 50 degrees south latitude. You can even do things you couldn't do if you were there, like change the color of the landscape, break it down into shades of gray, or reshape it—moving down and up in resolution, stretching and compressing geographical features to bring out hidden details. You can also zoom in on details, boosting magnification from eight to sixty-four times normal. If you find an image you particularly like, you can save it, and use it with other graphics programs.

Mars Explorer isn't the personal space cruiser we were promised after Gagarin and Shepard took their rides, but it will do until the real thing comes along.

Miss Tiffany's Guide to Looking Unusual

by Tiffany Lee Brown

General Clothes

If classic, sturdy clothing in rugged fabrics makes your heart pound with pleasure, move beyond the overpriced trendiness of Tweeds, and L.L. Bean. Genuine Amish-wear in simple cuts has been sold by the **Gohn Brothers** for 90 years, and they sell bolts of cotton and a wide selection of inexpensive rubber boots, too. Don't expect pictures, though; the catalogue is as ascetic as the Amish lifestyle (Gohn Bros., Box 11, Middlebury, IN 46540-0111; 219-825-2400).

Whimsical, sexy fashions borrow deathrock club fabrics like black lace and thick clingy stretch cotton/Lycra, cutting them into the latest trendy shapes at one of the most irresistible boutiques on the Upper Haight: **Backseat Betty**. Some of their wares can be purchased through the mail (Backseat Betty, 1780 Haight Street, San Francisco, CA 94117; 415-387-9819).

Girl, if you haven't found **Vernon's** yet, you haven't lived! There really is something for everyone in this charmingly retro-looking catalogue, but it's downright indispensable for the larger-bodied. Clip-on earrings, makeup kits, wigs, breast prostheses, gaffs for hiding the male genitalia beneath scanty panties, all manner of corset and girdle, stretch lace lingerie, petticoats, and hosiery are featured along with reasonably-priced fetish gear for all genders, and lots of panties. (Vernon's Specialties, 386 Moody St. Waltham, MA 02154; 617-894-1744; fax 617-647-4082).

Fetish/Leather

Those with a medieval bent and deep pockets should send $3 for **St. Michael's** catalogue. Forget your inner child; unleash your inner Arthur or sultry dungeon maiden in St. Michael's armor and corsets. Drape the dark knight of your soul in handmade leather attire, or mask your secret Executioner. (St. Michael's Emporium,156 East Second St., Suite 1, NY, NY 10009; 212-995-8359). To complete the neo-Dark-Ages wardrobe, chainmail fashions are available from Dungeon Wear (7661 Melrose Ave. LA, CA, 90046; $2 for catalogue).

Featuring cock harnesses, fetish jockstraps, men's harnesses, and enema equipment, **A Taste of Leather** aims more at the boys than

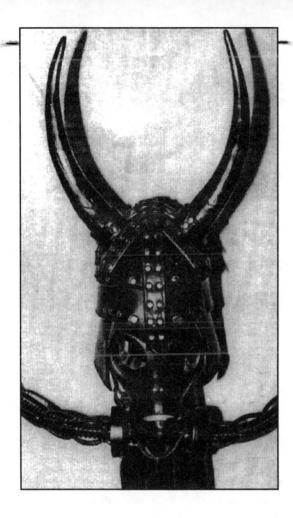

Firedrake Battle Helmet from St. Michael's Emporium. Photo © St. Michael's Emporium

the grrrls, but does include some women's gear and a selection of dildos for everyone (317A 10th St., San Francisco, CA 94103; 800-367-0786;415-777-4643). Then again, your idea of leather may be a simple, generic biker jacket. If you want one cheap, call 800-55-CRAMP.

Industrial Fetish Gear

Nylon-webbing harnesses made for firefighters on the rescue. Kevlar-lined frisking gloves. Biohazard protective wear, like masks and poly-ethylene coveralls. If the genuine occupational accessories of cops and public safety experts excite you more than plain old leather, you must have this catalogue. Be sure to sound legit when you call in, though; be creative—or try telling them you're an EMT (Emergency Medical Technician). (**Gall's Buyer's Guide**, P.O. Box 554308, Lexington, KY 40555-4308; 800-477-7766). If that falls through, take a gander at the latex, gas masks, and gloves at **Lab Safety** (Lab Safety Supply Inc., P.O. Box 1368 Janesville, WI 53547-9953).

Accessories

Are you stranded in Bumfuck, Nowhere, without an acceptable variety of bright, unnatural hair dyes? Or like me, are you just too lazy to leave the house for makeup, t-shirts, and accessories? **Nosferatu Productions** provides an array of Goth basics, including books and music (Nosferatu Productions, P.O. Box 3535 Hollywood, CA 90078; $1 for catalogue). For hard-to-find coffin purses, write to **Wicked Ways**; they also sell jewelry, boots, and pvc/latex/rubber gear (Wicked Ways P.O. Box 16752, Alexandria, VA 22303; 703-379-4735). Thanks to **Siren**, Canadian Goths don't have to cross the border for clothes and accessories, either (Siren 463, Queen St. W., Toronto, Ont. M5V 2A9, Canada; 416-363-9288).

Jewelry

A select (and expensive) stock of sterling silver-barbed and thorned crosses vies with the preserved parts of real bats at **Empire of the Damned** (P.O. Box 20360 NY, NY 10009). For the Wiccan in every girl, there's the faerie- and rune-infested **Medusa's Circle**, which sells clothing, jewelry, and magick toys (1491 Washington Ave., Miami Beach, FL 33139; 305-532-1882).

If you're looking for body jewelry, **Silver Anchor** creates consistently superb surgical stainless steel pieces for every piercing need imaginable. In addition to a helpful, funny staff who don't talk down to novices, they provide needle holders, replacement hematite for captive bead rings, drilled stainless balls for barbells, custom skull designs, septum retainers, instant topical freeze spray, and shackles (their clamps, ring closers, and forceps are pricey, so you might want to purchase those elsewhere). Their three- and five-ball cascading circular barbells might be the most aesthetically pleasing drop of steel I've ever seen on a pair of nipples (the 14-gauge, 1/2" width look especially well-proportioned), but they're worth the price even if you just want to adorn your ears (Silver Anchor Enterprises, 800-848-7464).

Famous for their salons in San Francisco and Los Angeles, **Gauntlet** mail order offers a glossy, information-heavy catalogue. Gold specialty pieces shaped as nuts-and-bolts, horseshoes, Cupid's arrows, and a stunning "Sunburst" shield to surround the nipple are available in addition to more traditional pieces and supplies. Extremely valuable to the piercing newbie or to the terminally curious, they sell back issues of *Piercing Fans International Quarterly* as well (Gauntlet Enterprises, 8720 Santa Monica Blvd., LA, CA 90069; 213-657-6677).

Fuck-me footwear
from the Pierre
Silber catalog.

Shoes

The staple of Doc Marten-wearing subcultures for years, **NaNa** is still around and selling a solid array of boots and shoes (NaNa, 800-347-4728).

For a no-nonsense approach to pricey fantasy shoes, ask for **Pierre Silber's** catalogue. A formidable spectrum of fuck-me footwear—thigh-high boots, six-inch ankle wrap spikes, lock pumps, feathered boudoir heels, and wicked slingbacks—fits on the single, innocent-looking page you'll receive in the mail. And listen up, boys and girls: most products come in sizes 5 through 15W (Pierre Silber, P.O. Box 265 Saratoga, CA 95071-0265; 408-735-7605; fax 408-735-0727).

Even hippies need shoes sometimes, which is why Birkenstocks exist. The quintessential granola shoe is now available in many colors, styles, and sizes (**Barrett's Birkenstock**, 1471-J Pomona Rd., Corona, CA 91720; 909-371-2860).

Cellular Hackers' Master Reference

information from: DYNASPEK, 16835 W. Bernardo Dr., #201, San Diego, CA 92127

Let's get one thing straight: the unnamed authors of this book do not advocate or endorse hacking into cellular phone calls. No sir. This is an educational tool and repair guide for cellular phone operators, hobbyists and phreakers, er...I mean fans.

Topics covered include general operating data, cellular switching systems and terms, Numeric Assignment Module info, and discovering the ESN of a cellular phone. There is also a cell phone buyer's guide, publication recommendations, FCC information, area codes for the U.S. and Canada, programming instructions, cellular frequency channel lists and control channel data stream data for... extreme fans. But not phreakers.

THE
PIRATE RADIO
DIRECTORY
by George Zeller
and Andrew Yoder

1993 Edition

Tiare Publications

The Pirate Radio Directory

$14.95 ppd ($15.95 foreign) from: Tiare Publications, P.O. Box 493, Lake Geneva, WI 53147; 800-420-0579

An annual guide to pirate radio broadcasting. Entries include all the information possible on broadcast frequencies, formats, and QSL addresses. Entries can range anywhere from a few sentences for really obscure (or frequently silent) stations to big, encyclopedic

Wire Line Radio

Wire Line Radio, which also identifies itself with the WLR call letter, began its pirate broadcasting career in August 1991. In 1992, it was active on a few subsequent occasions in the 7415-kHz area at times between 2300 and 0500 UTC. WLR normally features light rock and pop music with older prerecorded comedy skits from such artists as Lenny Bruce, Rusty Warren, and The Firesign Theater. One favorite article for the station operator to read over the air is "Scrotum Self Repair." The station became more active in 1993, with broadcasts occurring primarily on frequencies between 7423 and 7561 kHz. Wire Line Radio is now using considerably more power than in the past--often as much as 1,500 watts AM output, so it can be heard across all North America (V-Post Office Box 109, Blue Ridge Summit, Pennsylvania 17214; R-A).

The No Metal, No Rap, No Crap, Pirate On Your 41, 19 Meter and MW Dial

WIRE LINE RADI

from **The Pirate Radio Directory**

entries for (in)famous pirate broadcasters.

The book also contains an index of all the pirate stations mentioned in previous editions of **The Pirate Radio Directory.** Yes, previous editions, going back to 1989, are available from Tiare; their catalog is $1 from the address above.

FM MicroPower Radio Guide

$15 ppd ($17 foreign) from: mycal, P.O. Box 750381, Petaluma, CA 94975-0381; email: mycal@netacsys.com

If you ever wanted to build and run your own clandestine radio station, everything you need to know to get started is in this one 44-page packet: plans for amps, antenna design, modifications of stock equipment that will let you broadcast, as well as plans for power supply, powermeter, dummy load, compressor and limitor. Also, FCC information.

Interested radio hackers should note that mycal, the author, is willing to trade the **FM MicroPower Radio Guide** for hard information.

Radio Hardware Suppliers

Universal Radio

catalog free from: Universal Radio, 1280 Aida Dr., Reynoldsburg, OH 43068; 800-431-3939; fax 614-866-2339

Equipment for shortwave and amateur radio, as well as scanner enthusiasts. Transceivers, antennae, headphones, books, and parts. They carry home and portable gear, and have some used equipment, too.

Pan-Com International

catalog $1 from: Panaxis Productions, P.O. Box 130, Paradise, CA 95967-0130; 916-534-0417

A huge assortment of video and audio broadcast, receiving and monitoring gear. Surveillance and countersurveillance gear. Books and zines. Plus, electronic hobby kits, car amps, and weird science kits such as Van de Graaff generators and Tesla coils. Fun for the whole wired family.

The first Greyhound bus equipped with a 2-way radio leaves a Chicago station during the company's 1945 test; from *Popular Communications*

Popular Communications

$21.50/year (12 issues; Canada/Mexico $24.00; overseas $26) from: Popular Communications, 76 N. Broadway, Hicksville, NY 11801-9962

Cellular phones, CBs, satellite communication and old radio shows are the story here. Tech columns share space with general communications news. In one issue, they reported on the PCS challenge to cellular phones, Chinese pop music radio, a look at old wireless broadcasting, and lots of products reviews. A monthly column also keeps you up to date on what's happening inside the FCC.

Monitoring Times

$19.95/year (12 issues; foreign $28.50) from: Monitoring Times, P.O. Box 98, Brasstown, NC 28902-0098

Monitoring Times covers virtually everything you can do with radio frequencies, including scanning, shortwave, satellite TV long-distance listening, etc. They publish columns for beginning hams, radio experimenters, review equipment, discuss antennae, frequency guides, etc. Also, lots of great ads.

Reclaiming the Airwaves

information with SASE from: Free Radio Berkeley, 1442 A Walnut St., #406, Berkeley, CA 94709

Micropower radio advocates and activists come together in this zine that's both a newsletter, keeping you up to date on pirate and micropower stations in the U.S. and around the world, but it's also a tool (and call) for action. Produced by Free Radio Berkeley, **Reclaiming the Airwaves** happily defies the FCC and their tight regulation of the airwaves. Toward this, the zine sells transmitter kits, amps, etc., to encourage fellow troublemakers to get on the air.

• *AVOIDING THE FCC*

To dispel one rather dated myth, triangulation using three vehicles to locate a transmitter is no longer a technique used by the FCC. Nor do they drive around in bright orange trucks with the letters FCC on them, if only it was that simple. Instead, they use only one vehicle (a white Chevy Suburban in SF Bay area) which has been heavily modified with extremely expensive high tech gear. In most cases the metal roof has been replaced with a plastic roof to match the original one. Embedded within it is a group of antennas known as a doppler radio direction finding array. With this they can derive the bearing of the target transmitter....

Due to the nature of the direction finding equipment used, they can get pretty close to where a transmitter is operating. However, their gear can not lead them directly to the unit. Instead, they look for visual clues, antenna, cars with political bumper stickers, etc. If you minimize the clues, you minimize the risk.

Radio Resistor's Bulletin

information from: RRB, P.O. Box 3038, Bellingham, WA 98227-3038; email: haulgren@well.sf.ca.us

A grassroots group that grew out of the struggle between community radio advocates and the trustees of Western Washington University in Bellingham. Eventually, the local radio resistors won their battle, but the newsletter they created to keep the community informed about the battle is still alive, bigger and broader than ever. **Radio Resistor's Bulletin** is intended as "a newsletter that could serve as a conduit for information between volunteers at other non-commercial stations." The editors are in touch with local radio stations and pirates through the U.S., Europe, Canada, and Asia. You won't learn to hack the airwaves here, but you can hear the voices and see the ideas of people who want to keep radio as open and freeform as possible.

Miss Vera's Finishing School
For Boys Who Want To Be Girls

Veronica Vera, Dean of Students   212/242-6449
Paulette Powell, Dean of Cosmetology

Miss Vera's Finishing School For Boys Who Want To Be Girls

information from: Miss Vera's Finishing School, P.O. Box 1331, Old Chelsea Station, NY, NY 10011; 212-242-6449

For the girl that lurks (in slingback pumps and a cocktail dress) in the heart of every boy, there's Miss Vera's training academy for cross-dressing. With a variety of courses to choose from, Miss Vera and her lady teachers can probably fill the needs of all aspiring gender-fuckers. You can start with the Sensuality Seminar, a two-and-half hour bodywork and make-over session. It starts with a dedication ritual to the new you, a massage, tips on make-up application, posture and poise, and ends with you fully dressed and done up right. This basic class is $300.

Other classes offered include corset training, a fashion course, make-up (with a video lab), flirting, French maid training, and ballet. You can also go on an evening field trip (in your best gown, of course) with Miss Vera and another teacher, or join the class for a pajama party.

Some classes are a few hours, some a few weeks. None are cheap, but Miss Vera doesn't apologize for that. She knows her job, and does it well. She's also something of a disciplinarian, even when it comes to money. "All fees," she says, "must be tendered in crisp, clean bills in a pink envelope." So, are you man enough for cha-cha heels?

Selfloving: Video Portrait of A Women's Sexuality Seminar

$45 ppd (make checks payable to Betty Dodson) from: Betty Dodson, P.O. Box 1933, Murray Hill, NY, NY 10156

Betty Dodson is part sex cheerleader, part educator, part shamaness. She uses her own experience to teach women how to masturbate—and something more. By teaching women to take control of their own pleasure and their bodies, she's teaching them basic ways to change their lives.

This video is a document of one of Betty's workshops. You see the women (young and old, fat and thin) arrive, nervously undress, and through the course of the seminar, become relaxed and more confident. Dodson herself uses a combination of Dale Carnegie "You can do it!" inspiration, as well as practical physical advice on masturbation techniques to take these women to places many of them had never been before.—Andrea Reich

Solo Sex: Advanced Techniques

$12.95/year (4 issues) from: Factor Press, P.O. Box 8888, Mobile, AL 36689; voice/fax 205-380-0606

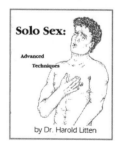

Solo Sex: Advanced Techniques by Dr. Harold Litten

For every guy who's ever dated his right hand (or left, for you southpaws), here's a how-to guide that proves you can teach an old dog new tricks. **Solo Sex** is a masturbation manual for men, pure and simple. Why, you ask, do you need a book to tell you how to do what comes so naturally? Well, maybe there are other ways to do it. Maybe there are techniques and tricks that not only feel better than whatever it is you're doing now, but are better for you.

Not only does **Solo Sex** cover the basic moves of a one-handed love fest, but it uses text and illustrations to show you such tricks as intensifying your orgasms, having multiple orgasms, how to have an orgasm simply by thinking about it, and how to use toys like vacuum pumps and vibrator cups. Best of all, the book is ring-bound, so it will stay open, leaving your hands free to play the home version of the game.

As sort of an ongoing technique and discussion forum, *Celebrate the Self* is a quarterly newsletter that grew out of **Solo Sex.** It features letters and tricks from readers, as well as reviews of toys, videos and books.

Wondrous Vulva Puppet

$80 ppd (CA residents add sales tax) from: House 'O Chicks, 2215-R Market St., #813, San Francisco, CA 94114; 415-861-9849

A woman friend once told me about how one night in bed, after her boyfriend had been slurping around for awhile between her thighs, she grabbed him by the hair and yelled, "There's the clit, you moron!" (or words to that effect). For any woman who's ever wondered about her own genital construction, or for any woman with a lover (or even a curious kid) who's clueless anatomy-wise, we introduce the Wondrous Vulva Puppet.

The puppet is hand-stitched and made of soft materials, such as velvet and satin. It's shaped roughly like a catcher's mitt, and is anatomically correct, from the outer lips of the labia majora, to the protruding clitoris, all the way to the G-spot (somewhere around your middle finger). Accompanying the puppet is a map showing the names and locations of the erogenous zones of a real-life vulva.

Whether you're teaching a group of kids a biology lesson, or amusing a lover by having the puppet tell jokes (yes, you can make it open and close like a big, plush clam), the vulva puppet is truly wondrous.

Pleasure Plus

information from: Good Vibrations, 938 Howard, #101, SF, CA 94103; 415-974-8990; fax 415-974-8989

Speaking as someone with a penis, condoms suck. But in an age when STDs can kill you deader than a stuffed bear in a storage locker behind an abandoned filling station on one of those unmaintained sections of Route 66, condoms make sense.

Whine no more, boys; **Pleasure Plus** condoms are here! The secret of the **Pleasure Plus** is the design on its head: it's balloon-shaped, like one of the Montgolfier Brothers' hot air balloons. This extra latex is up front around the head of your penis creating friction where it counts the most. **Pleasure Plus** are more expensive than other condoms, but after test-driving one, I think you'll agree that they're worth it.

Floggers

Heartwood Whips of Passion

catalog $5 from: Heartwood Whips of Passion, 412 N. Coast Hwy., #210, Laguna Beach, CA 92651; 714-376-9558

Not only is this is a well-rounded catalog full of well made whips, cats, riding crops, paddles etc., but it's also a mini-introduction to the leather

Colorful horse hair floggers from Heartwood

world. At the front is a listing of leather events, and further on is a history of whip-making, and even a short primer on the proper (and safe) way to spank those bad girls and boys who really deserve it.

Sorodz

catalog $2 from: Sorodz, P.O. Box 10692, Oakland, CA 94610; 510-839-2588

Divided into sections on rubber whips, horsehair whips, paddles, rods, batons and "beyond," the Sorodz catalog has something for almost every flagging need. From small, lightweight whips that are more stimulating than painful, to high-impact white plastic rods for those Singapore graffiti-writing punishment fantasies; they also carry such exotica as a Victorian-style paddle with a teardrop shaped loop for a head, a full 20" horse tail attached to a medium butt-plug, and the postmodern "Little Smacker," a clear plastic whip that's mostly a stinger, but with a powerful sound.

Adam & Gillian

information from: Adam & Gillian, c/o The Utopian Network, P.O. Box 1146, NY, NY 10156; 212-686-5248 weekends, 516-842-1711 weekdays

Like all fine craftmanship, A&G's wonderful whips and canes satisfy both utilitarian and aesthetic criteria. Conveniently labeled with tags like "Very Gentle" and "Ultra Savage," the selection ranges from "soft and sensual" nylon or leather whips ($40-$195) to the "serious stuff" pages featuring leather cats, straps of laminated industrial belting, and neoprene rubber slappers ($20-$260). Nipple cuffs, for women who want the effect without the actual nipple piercing, are sold along with charms and handcuff-shaped jewelry.—Tiffany Lee Brown

Software via FTP

For some interesting, wacky or just plain strange stuff on the Net check out these sources:

The Emperor Norton Utilities

The Emperor Norton Utilities is not an organized collection of software by anybody's definition. It is a slapdash hodge-podge of weird and eristic programs. It contains all sorts of programs for all sorts of computers, and no two people are likely to agree on what is in the Utilities. The Emperor Norton Utilities FTP site contains but a small (but constantly growing) sample of the Utilities.

These pieces were written by many people. I wrote mcelwaine, beable and kibo (three text filters). Jer Johnson wrote Xtacy and ddate. Most of the programs on the site consist of C source code. Two of these require the X window system running on something UNIX-like. As soon as I find programs for other machines that fit on the site, I will add them.—Joseph Matheny

FTP: yoyo.cc.monash.edu.au:/listserv/flat-earth/norton

The Process Media Lab

The FTP site has been created by The Process Media Lab in tandem with their creation of a multimedia visual project with the music group, Skinny Puppy. The site provides the Internet user with an ongoing interactive art forum that is currently concerned with this project. Images, sounds, texts, and animations that have been created by core Process members, as well as the virtual audience, are available for download.

It should be noted that The Process is a collective experience and all contributions (uploads) will work towards defining the aesthetic of The Process itself.

The Process also strives to provide the Net audience with an enlightened viewpoint in the field of anomalous research. Areas within the FTP site relate to topics such as Non-Lethal Weapons Research, Remote Viewing, The UFO Conspiracy and promoting Media Literacy.—Joseph Matheny

FTP: ftp netcom.com look in /pub/puppy

Cool Mac Stuff

Connectix's RAM Doubler software sounds too good to be true, but it actually works. Just pop this program into your System folder, restart and bang! Your RAM is doubled. It's that simple. And unlike Apple's virtual memory, the extra RAM doesn't kick in unless you're right at the point of running out of memory, so it doesn't drag your whole system into a glacially-slow state. RAM Doubler doesn't work with all Macs. You need at least 4 MB of RAM and a 68030 or higher processor that supports virtual memory. The software retails for around $99. (Information from: Connectix Corp., 2600 Campus Dr., San Mateo, CA 94403; 800-950-5880; 415-571-5100; fax 415-571-5195)

If you have a laser printer, Toner Tuner is a terrific money saver. Just install TT and every time you hit "Command P," you get a print screen with a ribbon control at the bottom. By moving your cursor along the ribbon, you can specify how much toner you want the printer to use for each job, from 0% to 100%. For draft copies, I've found that I can get perfectly readable copies using between 40% and 60%. This will save a lot of toner cartridges in the long run. Toner Tuner is about $25 retail. (information from: Working Software, P.O. Box 1844, Santa Cruz, CA 95061-1844; 408-423-5696; fax 408-423-5699; email: CompuServe 76004,2072)

LaserWriter "LaserWriter II NT"			7.1.2	**Print**
Copies: 1	**Pages:** ⦿ All ○ From:	To:		**Cancel**
Cover Page: ⦿ No ○ First Page ○ Last Page				
Paper Source: ⦿ Paper Cassette ○ Manual Feed				
Print: ⦿ Black & White ○ Color/Grayscale				
Destination: ⦿ Printer ○ PostScript® File				
Toner Tuner™ [About...] ◄ ▦ ► 65 % ☒ Use T.T.				
Section Range: From: 1 **To:** 1 ☐ Print Selection Only				
☐ Print Hidden Text ☐ Print Next File ☐ Print Back To Front				

To save those floppy drives—the ones that collect dust, cat hair, and Oreo crumbs, try Drive Cleaner! by Seven Hills Software. It comes with software, a cleaning disc and fluid. It's even Apple-approved, so you know it won't realign your heads into cookie-cutters. About $30. (information from: Seven Hills Software, 2310 Oxford Rd., Tallahassee, FL 32304-3930; 904-575-0566; fax 904-575-2015; email: CompuServe 75300,1743)

PornoWriter

for Macintosh; $10 ppd (make checks payable to Robert Carr) from: Smurfs in Hell, P.O. Box 2761, Borah Station, Boise, ID 83701

Ever read those porn magazine letters columns where (alleged) readers write in about their (alleged) sexual antics? Even though you know they're a pack of lies, they still make you feel like a slug because these people even lie better than you. Well, now the pain is over. **PornoWriter** is software for anyone who's ever wanted to fire off a pornographic tall tale but never quite got around to it.

Open up **PornoWriter** and it gives you a couple of scenarios to choose from. It then creates outrageously complicated and physically impossible fables for you to indulge in. For instance, choose the "Clapp Twins" and you might get: *Lisa was amoral and almost a double for Klaus Barbie! Jessica was brain dead and had the biggest pair of tits I'd ever seen!...Late one night as I was taking care of some unfinished embalming, there was a knock at the door...* Along with the canned scenarios, **PornoWriter** features a wonderful range of absurd sound effects, including rants from Jerry Falwell and songs by Mr. Rogers. You really can't program *PornoWriter*, it just spews out scenes from the topic you select; but for ten bucks, it's a steal.

PixelPlay

for Macintosh and Windows; information from: Silicon Sports, 324 St., Palo Alto, CA 94301; 415-327-7900; fax 415-327-7962
(Macintosh requirements: Macintosh SE/30 or higher; System 6.0.7 or later; 4 MB RAM; QuickTime 1.0 or later)

PixelPlay lets you use any combo of QuickTime movies as a screen saver. You can use it as a stand-alone program or as an After Dark module. As a test, I lifted some clips from a CD-ROM encyclopedia. Now when my monitor blacks out, I get Amelia Earhart, Jackie

Gleason going ballistic in **The Honeymooners,** the Hindenburg disaster, Lenin making a speech, a praying mantis eating a beetle, and the lunar module landing on the moon.

For folks without CD-ROMs to crib from, **PixelPlay** comes bundled with a load of its own movies: sports images, tourist spots, animals, cars, etc. The Mac version retails for around $50 and the Windows for around $60.

Encryption

Stego
For Macintosh

First there was PGP, now next big step in data protection is here—and it's cheap. **Stego** is a software tool that takes your encrypted messages and hides them inside PICT image files. In other words, no one has to know that you have any encrypted files on your system. By hiding messages inside images, you get double the protection of standard encryption. First, a snoop has to know that there's hidden data inside a normal-looking image file, and second, the snoop then has to crack the encryption code of the file itself.

Like PGP, you can get a Macintosh-compatible (PC and other versions are under development) of **Stego** free from the following anonymous FTP site: sumex-aim.stanford.edu. Check the Infomac/Recent directory. If you want **Stego** updates and additional features, you can register it with Romana Machado, its author, for $15. You can contact her via email: romana@apple.com.

Dolphin Encrypt
for MS-DOS and Windows: information from: Dolphin Software, 48 Shattuck Sq., #147, Berkeley, CA 94704; 510-464-3009

Dolphin Software produces several types of encryption software. For most uses, **Dolphin Encrypt** does nicely. It's a symmetric-key program that cloaks data using the key you specify, from 10 to 60 characters long. You can encrypt multiples in different subdirectories with a single command. You can output the encrypted file as binary or text. There is also a more butch version of the program, called **Dolphin Encrypt Advanced**, and an ultra easy-to-use program **EZ-Crypt** that works mostly in the background. **Dolphin Encrypt** and **Decrypt** together run around $160.

A UFO Primer

by Virginia Bennett

1993; 29 pp.
$5.20 ppd (CA residents add sales tax) from:
Regent Press, 6020-A Adeline, Oakland, CA
94608; 510-547-7602; fax 510-547-6357

You won't find a better book to get you up to speed on the basic facts, theories, terms and images associated with UFOs. In simple, clear language (remember those kids' encyclopedias you used to copy your reports from?), Bennett lays out the basic schema of the UFO world, from the Roswell incident to animal mutilations, to abduction reports, to the infamous Men in Black. This concise book also has two appendices, one explaining "close encounter categories," and the other a recommended reading list. A fine book, that's also brief enough that you can finish it in a single sitting.

Photo: Augusto Arrandz, March 1967, Yungay, Peru; from A UFO Primer.

Area 51 Viewer's Guide

by Glenn Campbell

1993; 116 pp.
$18.50 ppd (NV residents add sales tax; Canada/Mexico $19.50; overseas $25) from: Secrecy Oversight Council; HCR Box 38, Rachel, NV 89001

A simple, self-published guidebook that will get you acquainted not only with the background of Area 51, but up close and personal with the place itself. The **Area 51 Viewer's Guide** includes milepost logs, maps, and practical info on how to get your vehicle as close as possible to the Area 51 site without dying in the desert, or getting carted off to some federal dungeon.

For those who don't know what the hell Area 51 is, here's the deal: A UFO is any "unidentified flying object;" the designation doesn't mean something is from Neptune or the 9th dimension, it just means that you don't know what the hell it is. For years, odd aircraft have been spotted in and around the site known as Area 51. It doesn't mean that Martians have landed, but it probably does mean that there are aircraft tests going on, tests that your government doesn't want you to know about. The **Area 51 Viewer's Guide** is kind of a tourist guide to the World's Fair of Black Budget Aeronautics.

UFO Directory

edited by Alan H. Rubin

1993; 66 pp.
$18 ppd (CA residents add sales tax; Canada/Mexico $23; overseas
$28) from: Oasis Designs, 61159 El Coyote Lane, Joshua Tree, CA
92252; 619-366-8570; fax 619-366-8606

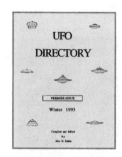

A kind of combination Yellow Pages, Chamber of Commerce listing,
Encyclopedia of Associations and Sears catalog rolled into one,
and all dedicated to getting UFO information into your hands. The
UFO Directory has listings for 192 groups, clubs, museums, stores,
etc. Aside from contact information, the **UFO Directory** gives you a
detailed description of each group, and tells you if it produces or
sells any UFO-related goods. The directory is also indexed by names,
acronyms, items (such as books, periodicals, videos, etc.),
researchers, broadcasters, and on and on. There are also five appendices, including a UFO bibliography and a UFO timeline.

UFO Zines

Far Out!

$9.95/year (4 issues; foreign $19.95) from: Far-Out! Magazine, P.O.
Box 16507, N. Hollywood, CA 91615-9955; 310-572-7272; fax
310-572-7264

"The Unexplainable, The Unusual, The Unreal." A glossy quarterly
that looks at a number of unexplained phenomena, with an emphasis on UFOs.

International UFO Library

$19.95/year (6 issues; foreign $8.95/issue) from: International UFO
Library, P.O. Box 461116, Escondido, CA 92046-9892

Fine graphics and decent writing set this zine apart from the pack.
Plus, each issue has a large catalog of UFO-related books and tapes.

UFO Newsletter

information from: UFO Info Club Int'l., P.O. Box 641691, LA, CA
90064-1691

Photocopied clippings concerning UFO-related events from newspa-
pers around the world. A membership publication.

UFO

for IBM and clones with Windows; information from: Software Marketing Corp. 9830 S. 51st St., Bldg. A-131, Phoenix, AZ 85044; 602-893-3377; fax 602-893-2042 (Requirements: 2 MB RAM; 256 color VGA; Windows 3.1 or higher; Microsoft compatible mouse and driver; CD-ROM drive and software; Soundboard recommended)

Anyone who wants to a chance to examine evidence of UFO sightings with the convenience and speed of a computer (not to mention the cross-referencing and graphics capabilities), should check out the *UFO* CD-ROM. Using a timeline that goes back 3,000 years, *UFO* gives you 1200 events to choose from. Each UFO event or sighting comes with a description, a longer narrative of the encounter, an image (where possible), and geographic information. You can search for UFO sightings by date, event or location. Some entries also include contact and abduction information. *UFO*'s graphics make it a unique package. Not only does the disc claim to have the "world's largest collection of UFO photographs" (and there are a lot), but it also includes video clips of UFO footage wherever possible.

UFOs: The Secret Evidence

$43.95 ppd (CA residents add sales tax) from: Lightworks, P.O. Box 661593, LA, CA 90066; 800-795-8273; 310-398-4949

Interviews with straight-arrow scientists and military officers gives this tape an air of seriousness and solidity often absent in UFO reportage. But the interviews are not the reason to get this tape: the UFO footage is. *UFOs: The Secret Evidence* contains 44 UFO film clips from NASA's archives and observers around the world. While these clips alone probably won't sway you either way, they make for compelling viewing.

UFO Organizations

The Flying Saucer Project

information from: The Flying Saucer Project, 956 Hamilton St., Allentown, PA 18101; 215-433-3610

"Museum and Alien Liaison Unit." A group dedicated to information and fostering good relations between earth-people and ETs. You can book guided tours of their museum in advance.

International UFO Center

information from: International UFO Center, P.O. Box 691388, Orlando, FL 32869; voice/fax 407-826-5294

A UFO museum and information center. Their catalog contains everything from obscure books to rubber stamps.

INTERNATIONAL

**UFO
CENTER**

Intruders Foundation

information from: Intruders Foundation, P.O. Box 30233, NY, NY 10011

A support and information group for UFO-abductees, their friends and family.

Project Blue Book

information from: PBB, 506 N. 2nd St., Ft. Smith, AR 72901; 501-782-7077

Now a private organization, this group of mostly military and federal investigators continues to gather and collate info on UFO incidents.

Project Starlight International

information from: PSI, P.O. Box 599, College Park, MD 20740

PSI is a group dedicated to documenting the presence of UFOs through observation with magnetometers, gravimeters, spectrometers, high-resolution optical scanners, etc. Not for buffs, but serious researchers.

Project to Research Objects, Theories, Extraterrestrials and Unusual Sightings

information from: PROTEUS, 274 2nd St., Elizabeth, NJ 07206

Not only is this group convinced that aliens exist, but they're researching the advanced physics the ETs use and how the physics might effect ordinary people.

Vehicle Internal Systems Investigative Team

information from: Project VISIT, P.O. Box 890327, Houston, TX 77289; 713-488-2884

A group of engineers, scientists and investigators who are researching the possible ways alien spacecraft might work. Their archives contain over 10,000 clippings, reports, and casebooks on UFO incidents.

Shooter's Bible

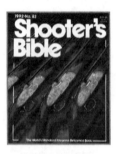

edited by William S. Jarrett et al
$18.95; Stoeger Publishing Co.
1994; 576 pp.

The basic reference book for civilian sport and hunting guns. It has sections on handguns, rifles, shotguns, black powder guns, sights and scopes, ammo, ballistics, and reloading. Each is listed with a photo, weight, ammo specs and, almost always, with its retail price. There's a reference section with book recommendations, a directory of gun makers and suppliers, a list of discontinued models and a list of gun, by caliber. Also included are articles on gun lore and history.

Laser Products

information from: Laser Products, 18300 Mt. Baldy Circle, Fountain Valley, CA 92708

For that science fiction-badass-Terminator look, nothing works better than a laser sight mounted on the front of a nasty handgun or rifle. Or if you don't want to go the laser route, how about an 11,000 candlepower tactical light? Laser Products makes and stocks them all, as well as the kits to attach them to your firearms.

Laser Products makes both flashlights and lasersights for all types of firearms. This is their 716 laser mounted on the fore-end of a Remington shotgun.

Scattergun Technologies

information from: Scattergun Technologies, P.O. Box 24517, Nashville, TN 37202; 615-254-1441; fax 615-254-1449

Urban Sniper Model, Item # 90132

- Remington 12 ga. 3" 1187P Magnum Parkerized Receiver with an 18" Rifled* Barrel

- Scout Optics with Extended Eye Relief

- Extended Magazine Tube, Total Capacity: 7 rounds

- Side Saddle Shell Carrier, Extended Capacity: 6 rounds (not shown, see page 41)

- Synthetic Buttstock and Fore Grip

- Adjustable and Collapsible Bipod

- High Visibility, Non-Binding Follower

- Performance Rated Magazine Tube Spring

- Jumbo Head Safety

- 3-Way Adjustable Action Sling (not shown, see page 42)

- Quick Detachable Steel Buttstock and Bipod Swivel

* For use with slugs only

Whether you want a new shotgun, or to retrofit an old one, Scattergun Technologies is the ultimate source for tactical shotgun tech. They take stock Remington 870 and 1187 model shotguns and rebuild them into tactical beasts—shortening the barrel to a home defense length of 18", installing a chromed safety switch that's easy to find (even in the dark) and installing a synthetic stock and recoil pad to save your shoulder. The S.G.T. Remington conversions also come with a "follower" (which shows you when the ammunition magazine is empty) and are "Parkerized" (a matte-black, non-glare finish). Other options include an extended ammo tube to let the gun hold more rounds, luminous sights, 5,000 and 11,000 candlepower aiming lights and a pistol-grip stock.

Crocodile Hunter

Anyone who expects to find themselves in the swamps of South or Central America, Australia, the Jungles of Borneo, Brazil or even the North Woods, will find that this "Crocodile Hunter" is big enough to takecare of their needs.

The knife has a full ten inch drop forged blade with blood groove on both sides. The handle is real India Stag, butt and double guillon hilt are solid brass. This is our own knife made for us on contract in Solingen, Germany. We have spared no expense. We have not scrimped on the steel but have used the best high-carbon stainless that can be drop forged. We offer no light weight alloy in fittings, but rather the very best brass. Having put no corners, we can only sell this knife direct to the user/collector. Not available to dealers.
10 1/4" clip blade, total length 15 1/4", brass butt and hilt, stag handle, weighs 1 lb. 2 oz., and comes with leather sheath.

AGCH-2 . . . . $124.95

Order by fax 24 hours a day 501-751-4520

800-255-9034

46

A quality horn-handle shiv, based on a Bowie Knife design, from A.G. Russell.

A.G. Russell

information from: A.G. Russell, 1705 Highway 71B North, Springdale, AK 72764; 800-255-9034; fax 501-751-4520

You won't find many knives below $50 here. A.G. Russell specializes in selling handmade knives for collectors. Companies they handle include Morseth, Randall, Dozier, and D'Holder. A decent selection of production and kitchen knives, too. They also sponsor a Knife Collector's Club.

The Edge Co.

information from: The Edge Co., P.O. Box 826, Brattleboro, VT 05302; 800-732-9976

A terrific selection of quality knives, from kitchen blades to push daggers, from 18" Bowie knives to a Gil Hibben Double Shadow: an 11" dagger that features a blade split into two 6" separate blades (like a forked tongue of polished silver). The prices are reasonable, too: you can get a small rollerball knife for as little as $11, or a replica of a medieval British sword for $229. They also carry videos, batons, stun guns, crossbows, CO_2 target pistols, etc.

Greene Military

information from: Greene Military, 7215 Kingston Pike, Knoxville, TN 37919; 800-521-7977; 615-588-5945

Mostly distributors of military and outdoor gear, they also have a small selection of survival and hunting knives. Also stun guns, pepper spray, batons, etc.

U.S. Cavalry

information from: U.S. Cavalry, 2855 Centennial Ave., Radcliff, KY 40160-9000; 800-777-7732; fax 502-352-0266

For the James Bond and/or Rambo in all of us, here's a catalog specializing in "military and adventure equipment." Lots of unusual blades here: matte-black machetes (for you night fighters), replicas of WWII German officer daggers, Gurkha knives, throwing knives, and a 23" folding knife called a Gypsy Navajo. They also carry such exotica as Zodiac boats, GPS gear, Soviet military watches, and night vision scopes.

Push Daggers

information from: The Edge Co., P.O. Box 826, Brattleboro, VT 05302; 800-732-9976

While they don't pack the visual punch of a Rottweiler-size hunting knife, or the exotic appeal of a square-nose *Tanto*, a push dagger is probably the most practical self-defense knife you can carry. What makes a push dagger unique is its T-shaped grip. This lets you fold your fingers over the crossbar of the "T" (as if you were making a fist), leaving the blade of the knife protruding from between your fingers. Unlike an ordinary knife, once you have a hold of a push dagger, it's hard to drop or for someone to knock it from your grasp (I've seen people keep their grip on the knife even after receiving a kick to the hand). This is an especially good knife for a woman, since in most self-defense situations, she will probably be facing someone bigger and stronger than her. Another reason that makes push daggers practical is that you can get them with blades short enough to be legal in many cities, but still long enough to cause pain in an opponent—which is all you need to do most of the time. Most push daggers are priced between $20 and $40.

The Institute of Blinding Light

catalog $5.45 from: The Institute of Blinding Light, 1101 Clay St., San Francisco, CA 94108

Your one-stop shopping catalog that will guarantee you a post-death trip straight to Hell. Of course, once you get there, all the other damned will think you're a real wag. Consider these items: the rubber crown of thorns, the do-it-yourself stigmata kit, snake-handling videos, "Altar Boys of the Catholic church" pin-up calendar, the Red Hot Gag Matzo, the "Ankles of Islamic Women" calendar, and stuff to piss-off every Buddhist, Hindu, Coptic and/or Zoroastrian on the planet.

By the way, the catalog itself is a memorable piece of folk art, hence the steep price, but think how much better you'll feel— after your miserable, slutty, drugged-out life—when you're roasting in the sulfur pits in the sixth circle of the Inferno and you can tell everyone, "Actually, I was a very nice person, I just bought this one lousy catalog and ended up here. Go figure"

Schwa

$15 ppd (catalog free with SASE) from: SCHWA, P.O. Box 6064, Reno, NV 89513

"Everything Not Strictly Forbidden Is Now Mandatory," announces a bumpersticker with the face of an extraterrestrial stamped on it. "Whatever Happens: DO NOT REACT," reads another. You don't have to be an alien conspiracy buff to appreciate the biting social commentary and unique iconic humour of Bill Barker's *Schwa* art-products. Culture-jamming slogans and thought-puzzles are disguised as toys, jewelry, and stickers in his stark black-and-white *Schwa* world, which is peopled by aliens (the

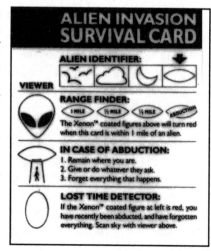

triangle-headed ones with big almond eyes, like in *Communion*) and stick figures. From glow-in-the-dark alien t-shirts to Alien Invasion Survival Card keyrings, everything Bill produces is irresistible, like finding a really neat toy at the bottom of a cereal box. Look beyond the giggly, pop-culture feel of these items and you'll also find serious, subversive art; it helps to have one or more of his books, which are included in the cheaply priced *Schwa* and *Counter-Schwa* "Kits."—Tiffany Lee Brown

Rene Cigler

information from: 213-871-5853

Make a down payment on the art collection you'll someday own by inquiring with Rene Cigler about the availability of the sculptor's renowned post-apocalyptic jewelry, cuffs, and other accessories made from wire, metal, leather, and baby dolls in bondage. Her work is also available from FringeWare, P.O. Box 49921, Austin, TX 78765; email: fringeware@io.com).—Tiffany Lee Brown

Grinder

information from: Grinder, P.O. Box 45182, Kansas City, MO 64171

Worthy of your respect as well as your money, Grinder epitomizes the best characteristics of underground mail order and distribution: lovingly-produced art, unique personality, hard work, a selective choice of products, and an eye for visceral detail. Although Grinder's John Bergin and James O'Barr may be moving up in the world, they still have the time and motivation to include their old and new works, along with other artists' output, in this slender catalogue. Bergin's industrial project, Trust Obey, has just signed to Nothing Records (Trent Reznor's label), but you can still obtain TO tapes for $5 or less; his work with the notable $C_{17}H_{19}NO_3$ collective is also sold along with other cyber/goth/industrial bands such as Caul and STG. I highly recommend back issues of Bergin's self-published comic zine, *Brain Dead,* and the book **Bone Saw**; also watch for **From Inside**, which Kitchen Sink Press releases this year. Grinder capitalizes on the print and film success of O'Barr's comic *The Crow* by offering a deluxe collectors' package with a signed hardcover book, CD, and a custom slipcase.—Tiffany Lee Brown

Catalogs A Go Go

Archie McPhee, P.O. Box 30852, Seattle, WA 98103; 206-782-2344; catalog free

In case there's anyone on the planet who hasn't heard about them, listen up. Archie McPhee is the ultimate toy-junk-weird-stuff-how-did-I-spend-so-much-money-on-rubber-snakes novelty store. Rubber lobsters and spiders; squirting things; fake tattoos; mannequin heads; squeezable globes; Hell money; Elvis playing cards, and much, much more!

Art Rat Enterprises, P.O. Box 16742, Chapel Hill, NC 27516-6742; catalog free

Erotic t-shirts, all black on white; designs by Hans Bellmer, Utamaro, Tom of Finland, Aubrey Beardsley, Egon Schiele, etc.

Artrock, 1153 Mission St., San Francisco, CA 94103; 415-255-7390; catalog free

Reproduction of mostly old Fillmore rock & roll posters; also carry posters of some newer bands: 7 Year Bitch, Butthole Surfers, Boss Hog, Urge Overkill.

Brainstorms, 8221 Kimball, Skokie, IL 60076; 800-231-7500; catalog free

Science and education kitsch for kids and grown ups. Toy robots; an electric pencil sharpener that looks like a gorilla head; lots of nice skeleton and body part t-shirts; glass eyes; Venus fly traps; mazes; astronomy gear, etc.

COTA Mailorder, 919 Aileen St., Oakland, CA 94608; catalog free

T-shirts: Scorpions, mystical symbols that actually look cool and austere rather than the usual New Age ecofluff, imaginative Goddesswear, a Mansonshirt, and a bold, encircled Chaos symbol.—T.L. Brown

Design Toscano, 15 E. Campbell St., Arlington Heights, IL 60005; 800-525-0733; catalog free

Gargoyles! For your mantle, bookcase, tabletop and lawn. Gargoyles that hold up tables, pictures or plants. Also some tapestries and death masks of famous dead guys. But mostly gargoyles!

Home Automation Laboratories, 5500 Highland Pkwy, #450, Symryna, GA 30082-5141; 800-466-3522; catalog free

Just how lazy are you? If you have the bucks, here's your chance to see. These guys sell amusing little boxes that you can hook to your computer—or use one at a time—that will let you automate just about every object in your home, from the curtains to the lights to the VCR. But my favorite items are the giant fake boulders that are really stereo speakers—for that postmodern luau look.

Lehman's Hardware & Appliances, P.O. Box 4779 Kidron Rd., Kidron, OH 44636; 216-857-5441; fax 216-857-5785; catalog $2

This catalog is dedicated to an Amish way of life; they carry dozens and dozens of non-electric appliances, wood stoves, propane and kerosene refrigerators, home butchering supplies and much more.

Seton Name Plate Co., P.O. Box JS-1331, New Haven, CT 06505; 800-243-6624; catalog free

Attractive wall coverings for you techno and industrial fetishists. Biohazard stickers; Radiation, laser and chemical warning signs; fluorescent traffic vests; traffic safety gear; weird OSHA tapes, etc.

Skeletons in the Closet, L.A. County, Dept. of Coroner, 1104 N. Mission Rd., LA, CA 90033; 213-343-0760; catalog free

Wacky trinkets from the LA coroner's office: t-shirt, tote-bag, beach towel, sweat shirt, watch, etc. Also a very cool lapel pin with the coroner's logo on it.

Twin Peaks Collectibles, Bruce Phillips, 46702 Camelia Dr., Canton, MI 48187; catalog free for SASE

Lots of out-of-production **Twin Peaks** items: collector's cards, books, zines, press kits, videos, British **Twin Peaks** board game, etc.

Where's the Art!!, 219 S.W. Ankeny, Portland, OR 97204; 503-226-3671; catalog free for SASE

From the folks who brought you the All Night Church of Elvis, this catalog features lots of original urban folk art: stickers, little dead Elvises in coffins, paper plates, pen holders, checkbook covers, earrings, Xmas ornaments, all with the King's mug on the front.

INDEX

INDEX

INDEX

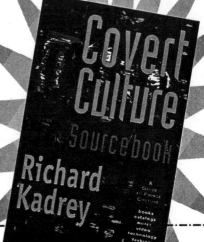